ANCHOR BOOKS

THE MIND IN RHYME

Edited by

Sarah Marshall

First published in Great Britain in 2004 by
ANCHOR BOOKS
Remus House,
Coltsfoot Drive,
Peterborough, PE2 9JX
Telephone (01733) 898102

All Rights Reserved

Copyright Contributors 2004

SB ISBN 1 84418 374 2

FOREWORD

Anchor Books is a small press, established in 1992, with the aim of promoting readable poetry to as wide an audience as possible.

We hope to establish an outlet for writers of poetry who may have struggled to see their work in print.

The poems presented here have been selected from many entries, and as always editing proved to be a difficult task.

I trust this selection will delight and please the authors and all those who enjoy reading poetry.

Sarah Marshall
Editor

CONTENTS

Don't Be A Victim	Natalie L West	1
Tommy	Jo Allen	2
At The Turning	Helen Marshall	4
A Night On The Tiles	Theresa M Carrier	5
Sunlight	J Adam	6
Look Into My Eyes	S J Olson	7
Umbrella Times	Darren Protherhoe	8
The Vase Of Roses	Michaela W Moore (Garlick)	9
Incandescence	John London	10
Switched On John	Denise K Mitchell	11
The Soul	Zaac Smart	12
A Thousand Brave Ghosts	Vernon Norman Wood	13
You Seem So Sleepy	Keith L Powell	14
Mind In Control	Beverley Odle	15
The Planet Of The Underworld	Indresh Umaichelvam	16
Just The Way I Feel	Elli Gibson	17
A Wish Is A Dream A Heart Makes	Sandra Griffiths	18
Waiting	Anthony Hull	19
Where Did It Go?	Meg Hoye	20
The Welsher	R Redi	21
Blend Me A Colour	Graham Jones	22
The World's Gone Mad	Judy Kerly	23
Foreign Country Foreign Land	Eleanor Lloyd	24
Picnic In The Park	Linda Meadows	25
The Pathway Of Life	Gillian Maynard	26
Our Earth	E M Minter	27
Betrayed	Melanie May	28
Windback Racer	Elizabeth Walker	29
But . . .	Charlotte Watkins	30
Getting Older	Jenny Wright	31
Forgotten Dreams	Jenny Winkworth	32
Unliked	Samantha E Whitehouse	33
A Dollshouse World	Tracy D wood	34
Sacrifice	Dennis F Tye	35
Carpe Diem	Peter Watson	36

The Intruder	Neil Warren	37
Fishing Boats	Kathleen Thorpe	38
My Angel Flew Away	B Taylor	39
The Day Begins	Ann Thompson	40
The Cry Of The Eagle	Brian L Porter	41
The Blue Tit	Valerie Mellor	42
Flutter By	Linda Lawrence	43
Beautify The Butterfly	William J Lyth	44
Restrained Secret	Katy M Lewis	45
Smile	Ali Rice	46
The Sound Of Your Silence	Andrew Ryan	47
On A Lazy Summer's Day	Jeff Slominski	48
You	Sophie Peppercorn	49
Nature Loving Boy	Graham Watkins	50
Nobody	Nadine Dudley	51
The Alternative Driving Test	Roger Williams	52
Fated Flight	Sue Umanski	53
Citizen's Unite	Lachlan Taylor	54
Punch-Drunk	Louis Foley	55
Two Candles In The Window	Kathleen Christine Bennett	56
This Is Me	Sheena Harris	57
Will You Be Mine?	Geoff Beatty	58
Soldiers Of Freedom	Kevin Kondol	59
Silence Is Not Golden	Marilyn Jones	60
Paradise	Margaret Waudby	61
The Deal	Gavin Capstick	62
Clouds	Doreen E Hampshire	64
Lifelong Love	Lesley Heath	65
Kirkwood Hospice	Brenda Brown	66
The Illegal Immigrants' Phrase-Book	John B Morris	67
Untitled	G Quinney	68
The Return Of The Last Of The Mohicans	Brian M Wood	69
Getting Old	R Claxton	70
Welcome Back	Maureen Arnold	71
Milestones Of Marriage	June Picken	72
My Love	Mel Price	73

I'm Going On Me Holidees!	Barbara Jackson	74
Warlord	A Sheard	75
That's My Boy	Janet L Smith	76
Quid	Sally Cocking	77
What Is?	Kate Elizabeth Shaw	78
Age	Gordon Ming-Li Ho	79
Tranquillity	Jacky Stevens	80
The Traveller	Christine Stallion	81
Untitled 2003	Lynne O'Connor	82
Dreams	Muriel Purdy	83
True Intent	Ron Powell	84
Technology	Michael Clenton	85
Soliloquy Of A Doomed Queen	Joseph Cope	86
When Are You Coming To Bed?	Jane Clarke	88
Walking	Paul F Clayton	89
Patio Panic	Janet Fludder	90
Lonely And Confused	M A Beckett	91
The Grand Jumble Sale	Patricia Burgess	92
Tots To Teens	Jacqui Beddow	93
Whispers	Jim Barnette	94
Bellybuttons	Paul Reynard	95
The Revered Pint	Allen Jessop	96
The Tears	E F Croker	97
Emotions	Della McGowan	98
A Tear I Cried	George S Johnstone	99
Fishy Forecasts Early 2003	Catherine Blackett	100
The Vampire	Deborah McDowall	101
The Postman	Bill Burkitt	102
Blood Ties	Anthony Welsh	103
Future	S A Almond	104
Shap Abbey	Katie Hale	105
Power	Ron Martin	106
Please Stop!	Annie Morrice	107
A New Kitchen	Rosalind M Walker	108
Suburbia	William McLellan	109
The Turbines	Trish Elliott	110
The Absence Of Love	L Finlayson	111
Advice To A New Recruit	Christine Skeer	112

The Little Church	Pauline Caton	113
Puppy's Thoughts	Rita Rogers	114
Sombre Thoughts	D T Pendit	115
Missing Mistress	Paul Bracken	116
The Bully Poem	Elizabeth Marsay	117
Roman Fort	Laura Thompson	118
The Wind Of Change	John Hoyland	119
Butterflies And Dragonflies	J Millington	120
Beaten By The Bully	Amanda Louise Marie Clarke	121
The D-Day Souvenir Supplement	Jane Hinchcliff	122
Timor Descendi	Sheila Anderson	123
Back Home Up North	Brian Williams	124
Homeless - Not Useless	A Sorley	125
Little Bit Of Heaven	Nigel W Davies	126
Extended Summertime In Orton	Eileen Todd	127
Travellers' Joy	R G Males	128
The Mask	Nicola Preston	129
The Heebie Jeebies	Keith Tissington	130
Solar Desire	Elizabeth M Rait	131
Take A Look Around	Craig Stewart	132
Purple Skirt	Margaret McKelvey	133
You Can't Win 'Em All	Roy Hare	134
Chasing The Dragons	Carol Kaye	136
A World For Us All	Peter Owen	137
Circumstances	I Morgan	138
A House By The Sea	Brendan McCauley	139
Favourite Things	Cate Ryan	140
Golden Wonders Of Gold Dust	Kiran Kaur Rana	141
Two Decades Of Love	Melanie McMahon	142
Bubbles	M Crowder	144
Velvet Moon	Marie A Golan	145
Life's Memories	Mary Veronica Ciarella Murray	146
A Dream	M Lyon	147
The Dawning Light Of Life	Patricia Johnson	148
Burning Bard	Lee Tellis Adams	149
Nostalgia	B Haworth	150
An Empty Space	Morgan Galsworthy	151

The Day	T B O'Brien-Barden	152
When All Seems Lost	Francis McGarry	153
Annihalation	Nancy Black	154
Jake	D Brown	155
Welcome Home	Dilys Hallam	156
Boat People	S M Thompson	157
As I Grow Older	Dorothy M Mitchell	158
Thank You For Caring For Us	Francesca Winson	159
Goodnight My Love	Mark Spiller	160
Being In Hospital For The Mentally Ill	Joanne Owen	161
Shattered Image	Tosky	162
Poorly Enriching Sweetener	Steven Ilchev	163
Light Transcending	Samantha Cumes	164
Tiny Alien	Audrey Luckhurst	165
Past, Present, Future	Lynne Gilbert	166
Words	Rhoda Starkey	167

DON'T BE A VICTIM

They start by stereotyping how you look
Seeing how far they can go
What they are doing to people inside
They really do not know.

Then they take it further
With pushing in a queue
A sly punch in the back
To make you feel really blue.

It's all about the power
And being in control
Making people think they're big and clever
Really they have no soul.

Don't let them push you over the edge
Don't bottle things up inside
Be brave and talk about it
Don't go running to hide.

Once you have released all that's inside
The clouds will start to clear
A light will shine at the end of the tunnel
You're no longer living in fear.

It's a happy life for you now
Stand strong and wear a grin
Remember you have a voice
Don't ever again be a victim.

Natalie L West

TOMMY

Never one to ride a horse -
Tommy was my first.
The Mews yard was my riding course
bareback, in trotting burst.

Dark brown hair, as I recall,
and tubby in the girth,
he was our carthorse, after all,
to ride him caused much mirth.

Dad drove from Bow to Stratford
next old trams' cavalcade,
to get the daily greens on board,
greengrocery was our trade.

Tram drivers were rather wary
of that old horse and cart,
'specially hand signals that vary
from my small arm pushed out.

Tommy plodded unaware
of trams' clanging concern,
Dad didn't know it was my dare
to signal a right turn!

Tommy was usually friendly
he lived in a makeshift shed.
We gave him oats a-plenty
and straw bales for his bed.

His hot breath and ordure
invaded our domain -
smell bearable in winter
but in summer like a drain!

He had one rather naughty whim -
he hated a surprise.
Once when I crawled beneath him
he hoofed me to the skies.

I'd only gone to fetch a ball
a friend had kicked inside,
but Tommy did not hear my call
and I was back outside!

For years while in short trousers
I proudly showed the scar.
My kneecap was a 'wowser'
to all except my ma!

Time came to move, our home to sell,
to bid him farewell was hard.
I hope Tommy went to a country dell
and not the knackers' yard.

Jo Allen

AT THE TURNING

Turn to me and pretend I matter,
Don't make me into who he used to be,
Look at me and make-believe you see,
Don't turn it all right back on me,
Speak my name if you remember it,
If you even notice my presence at all.
I may deserve it but I do not want this.

Touch me for more than the necessaries,
Don't make me into who he used to be,
Turn to me without turning me away,
Don't turn it all right back on me,
I thought you could make me believe again,
But now I see there is nothing worthy of my faith.
I may deserve it but I do not want this.

Don't make me into who he used to be,
Don't turn it all right back on me,
I may deserve it but I do not want this.

Helen Marshall

A Night On The Tiles

Hello Tabby Tiger are you back from your trail?
What on Earth is that stuck to your tail?
It looks like an ant and a big slimy snail,
Hold still now - I don't want to fail!

Who did you meet while you were out on the prowl?
Reynard the fox? Did he make you growl?
Oh, Big Ging, came and licked your food bowl bare
He gave me a look - huh! See if I care!

The best part of going out is coming home to me
Jumping up and going to sleep on my knee.
Night-time slips into morning, just you see
And when you wake, I'll have my cup of tea!

Theresa M Carrier

SUNLIGHT

All alone all by myself
Think of the part I put on the shelf
All the sorrow and all the tears
Amid the darkness filled with fears
Then came the sunlight bright
Shining and new
Giving my life a brand new view.

J Adam

LOOK INTO MY EYES

Look into my eyes and tell me what you see,
Do you see the youth I was, the child I used to be?
You see the man I am today,
The man who's lost the art of play,
One whose eyes have seen this world,
Through innocence that time's unfurled.

Look into my eyes and tell me what you see,
Can you see the man I am or one I want to be?
I want to feel a love of life,
Without the bitter twist of knife,
I long to feel life's gentle side,
Which way to turn I can't decide.

Look into my eyes and tell me what you see,
Can you see the man I am, one who must be free?
Untie these fetters let me breathe,
Let me go, my passions seethe,
Find me love, someone to hold,
Let not my heart become so cold.

S J Olson

Umbrella Times

No more rain
That's what I want to see,
Umbrella times
Are not made for me

Rain makes the mood
Darker than crimes,
We all want sunshine
Not umbrella times

Blame the rain
Rain makes people move away,
Bring me sunshine
Life without rain will make us pay

Umbrella times are here to stay
Whether we like it or not,
If it rains
Then let it be a lot

Darren Protherhoe

THE VASE OF ROSES

Once stood a vase of brightly coloured roses
full of life and sprightly spirited poses.
Positioned just right for all to see
the blooms seemed to call to me.

Such dashing beauty there on show
jaunty colours with flare and glow.
Some were in bud others in bloom
they provided such an aura in the room.

But something happened just for a while
the vase of beauty turned volatile.
What made such beauty turn so erratic
from the first extreme that was so erotic?

It seemed for a while they would demise
but the beauty was enough to suffice.
As it seemed that they would wilt
they appeared to sing a kind of lilt.

They lifted their heads in boastful fashion
as if suddenly filled with lustful passion.
Once again stands the vase in bloom
looking as peppery and effervescent again in the room.

Michaela W Moore (Garlick)

INCANDESCENCE

Oh rare! That incandescence
Glowing in the fading past
For me it is the essence
Of time that will ever last

Mem'ries formed when time began
Still hover captive, more so
Their impact mordant, and outran
The length which spread them below

Power feeding, upwards driv'n
The reason falling in place
The outer means contriven
With methods of inner space

The formula fades to smoke
The ashes thereof scatter
The history of some folk
Will so cherish the latter

The steeds that rush on headlong
As strides of progress today
Will right all the major wrong
That besets the ground for 'aye

John London

SWITCHED ON JOHN

Well John, the countries are almost gone,
The boundaries are torn away,
The world at this pace, is no longer a race,
For we travel by finger each day,
The love that you preached may not yet be reached,
But the barriers are starting to crumble,
The value of love, is finding its place,
Unlikely to ever tumble,
For greed without need, was planted as seed,
A thought that most will embrace now,
This transformation, less sixties information,
Could have been lost minus your know-how.

Denise K Mitchell

THE SOUL

The soul,
A hole.
It was cold,
Mould.
It was dark,
A mark.
A cold ground,
Where the souls lay safe and sound.

When the souls
Come out of their holes,
Searching for a body.
As body with its hobby,
The souls search, and search all day long.

And when they find the body,
With the hobby,
They sing out their happy song.

Zaac Smart (10)

A Thousand Brave Ghosts

A lone piper stands awaiting the dawn, on a rain soaked sodden hill,
Where the air is fresh and the pathway worn and, the rhododendrons still.
There's an eerie hush from the gathered clan, who stand in the trampled fern
Where the purple and white of the heather ran, all the way down to the burn.
In the distant mist, two lovers kissed
And, went their separate ways.
Then a beating drum, was heard by some,
As the lonesome piper plays.

O'er the brackened hills, where the skylarks nest and, the rabbits chase a doe,
Come the marching bands of the dead, at rest, piping tunes from long ago.
Through the highland hills, where the shepherds call and, the lambs follow a ewe,
A dirk is glinting, as the footsteps fall, when the tartan kilts pass through.
As a soldier dies, his lover cries
And, a bugle says farewell.
Then a bleeding heart, plays no more part,
As it marches off to Hell.

As a red deer feeds near the forest edge and, a waterfall cascades,
An eagle's eerie, sits high on a ledge, from where he makes his raids.
As he soars across where the dragoons lost, where the Fife and drums were played,
He pays no heed for the terrible cost, that the Scottish brave have paid
As a thousand ghosts, take up their posts,
You will hear the battle cry.
As all Scottish men, march through the glen,
Prepared this day to die.

Vernon Norman Wood

YOU SEEM SO SLEEPY

You seem so sleepy yes
As sleepy as can be
What on Earth do you dream of
When you fall asleep next to me.

You seem so sleepy yes
At this time of night
How do you manage to keep awake
Among so many bright lights.

You seem so sleepy yes
Well is it time for bed?
Yet once we get there you wake up
Do you want sex instead?

Keith L Powell

MIND IN CONTROL

I'm feeling trapped so very low
Not able to go back unable to step forward.
I feel so lost in a place unknown,
Detached from all that surrounds me so.

I feel such fear of all not known,
That once in time excited me so
Bored with what I have and do,
From this day onwards I could hide,
Say goodbye for good.

I think of how to be apart,
Of all what's living that surrounds my world,
It would seem as though I've been left behind,
By friends and family as they race forward in their lives.
Gone is my fighting spirit, it fails me now
At a time when it's most needed.

Caged am I - I pace to and fro
My mind it would seem out of control.
I am unrested in body, cold in soul
Low in spirits, yet no one knows.

Rewind and fast forward seems to be my mind,
Many emotions at one time,
Fear, sorrow and anger is to name but a few,
My thoughts of mind can this really be true?

To fear one's mind - and the depths it goes,
For your mind to have all control
Of emotions and life's it's as though
It's yourself you should fear most of all,
Not the outside world at all.

Beverley Odle

THE PLANET OF THE UNDERWORLD

'No one thinks of me,'
Says the forlorn planet
'I'm the smallest and darkest planet
No one knew I existed until seventy-three years ago
When people think of the universe
They think of eight jewels and a black stone

They associate the best of the Roman Gods
For the best eight planets
I am the god of the underworld
I have to make the longest orbit
It takes me two hundred and forty-eight years

I have no creatures or plants
No sun spots, no rings of ice
No one would care if a black hole swallowed me
Why did God create me?
I am a waste compared with the others

When I said this to my creator
God said, 'Everything and everyone has a purpose'
He said I was important to Him
Even though I was not important to anyone else
This is why I still make my very long trek around the sun.'

Indresh Umaichelvam (12)

JUST THE WAY I FEEL

A large black cloud covers the light,
You feel like you're losing a major fight,
You feel isolated, in a tiny space,
Like you're the only member of the human race.
You need an embrace, a quick one will do,
You need the comfort of a soothing cat's mew.
The story continues, turning the page,
It's like being trapped in a minute cage,
Then the light comes, it's over and done,
Then you just wait for the next time to come.

Elli Gibson

A Wish Is A Dream A Heart Makes

A wish is a dream a heart makes when no one else can hear,
A prayer of hope offered to a sky of twinkling stars?
A quiet gentle yearning of life without a care?
A hope to win the lottery or for peace upon the Earth?
A day without an argument and peaceful family life?

A wish is a dream a heart makes when no one else can hear,
What will I wish today in the stillness of my heart?
No illness coming to threaten routine of family life?
A bus that arrives on time against bad weathered odds?
A day of peace from war without famine or daily strife?

A wish is a dream a heart makes when no one else can hear,
But wishes can come true if we believe in them enough.
So I wish for wisdom and goodness in my soul,
I wish that I may *hear* what's in my children's hearts,
I wish for an open mind, not closed to others' plight.

A wish is a dream a heart makes when no one else can hear.
Wish becomes *miracle* when it turns true for you.
So say your wish out loud before you go to sleep.
Send your wish to Heaven into an angel's heart,
Then softly whisper *Amen* when you send your wish each night.

Sandra Griffiths

WAITING

When you are getting old and grey
death is lurking not far away.

You try to forget most of the time
but he is round the corner, hope you
over step the line.

He looks at the old gutter, that is
about to fall, the bus going too fast
the leaning wall.

We get past the lot, he shakes his head,
I will probably get him tomorrow
while he lays in bed.

Anthony Hull

WHERE DID IT GO?

Where did it go? My life? How long, for goodness sake?
Are there really ninety candles on this lovely birthday cake?
I can't be that old surely, I feel only forty-three,
Though sometimes act like seventy, for I'm older now you see.

My dancing days are over, well I cannot dance a reel,
But I like a gentle fox-trot, it depends on how I feel,
I used to love a polka, whirling round in double time,
But now I stick to waltzing since no longer in my prime.

I always put on make-up, it's the face that others see,
Tinted cream and lipstick and mascara, that's for me.
My hair already coloured to ensure no signs of grey
Since high heels flatter ankles, I'll wear them, come what may.

Where did it go? My life? It seems no time at all
Since mother sat me on her knee when I was very small.
Or when I was a schoolgirl with heavy braided hair,
How quickly all these years have passed, it really isn't fair.

I bought a car at twenty and I didn't need a test,
I loved that bull-nosed Austin, it simply was the best.
Today it's automatic and I only drive in town
For I do not like the motorways, the traffic gets me down.

My first love was a pilot who just flew off one day,
But other loves soon took his place, until my wedding day.
I loved my husband dearly and we watched our daughter grow
And she's a granny now herself, so where did that time go?

I've blown out all those candles though it took two puffs or more,
And I've waltzed around the ballroom and my feet are kind of sore,
So here I sit sedately, watch my birthday party flow,
Reflect that I am ninety! My life! Where did it go?

Meg Hoye

THE WELSHER

'People are living longer,'
sighed David Ivor Evans,
called 'Dai' for short.
His trade was funeral director
from a family of cadaver collectors,
he greeted the sick with a measuring stick.
Those damned cremations,
and their pinch-penny implications,
were knocking the bottoms
out of his coffins.
'Funerals are not what they used to be!'
mused the man from 'Plaid Cymru'.
When people start economising,
whims and choices were surprising.
Some even suggested canvas bags,
an impracticality because they sagged!
No more grand horses and hearses,
people think more of their purses.
So to boost up his trade,
in parlour window he displayed -
a bold notice to catch the eye
to direct any thoughts up to the sky.
The celestial notice read:
Hark! A message for the dying,
and in order for complying,
to be sure of a place in Heaven,
please bring them here to 'Die'.

R Redi

BLEND ME A COLOUR

Blend me a colour
A mixture of hues
Sweeten my sorrow
With rhythm and blues

Bend me and shape me
But keep me in mind
Label and tag me
For someone to find

Hope is a lost cause
A figment, a dream
Adrift in the silence
Where no one has been

A blind man can see
What others can't hear
Consumed by his thoughts
Of what others might fear

No one's immortal
And time passes on
So enjoy what you have
Before it's all gone.

Graham Jones

THE WORLD'S GONE MAD

Have you got an Ericsson, Motorola, Nokia?
Is yours a flip-top, vibrating camera?
How many texts do you send, by the way?
How many people have you spoken with today?

Have you got a Dell, Apple or a Laptop?
Pentium processor, numerous gigabytes.
Internet shopping, is the order okay?
You can sit by yourself in your little box all day.

Do you have a super woofer, recordable DVD?
Widescreen, surround sound, plasma TV?
Do you buy designer clothes from Armani or Gap?
Are you caught in the consumer trap?

For all of us some gadgets have to be had.
But the great divide with others can seem rather sad.
Keep up with the Jones' and occasionally hobnob,
Just be careful not to turn into a technological snob!

Judy Kerly

FOREIGN COUNTRY FOREIGN LAND

Foreign country, foreign land
It's hard to believe I am in England.
No different colour divideth me,
Only cruel thought and deed of jealousy.
For years I have tried to find
An answer to this trick of mind.

I used to sit and cry all night
And to my mind this is not right.
My body weak was no delight,
My mind, it seemed, had lost the fight.
I cannot go forward, cannot go back
For jealousy is on the attack.

How is one able to explain?
Jealousy only causes pain.
Your loved ones it can push away
They will not be back another day,
It can make you feel you are to blame,
The one that causes all the pain.

You must stand up and take the strain,
It is the only way to live again.
Everyone must have their goal
For life is not an easy stroll.
Future plans must come into play
Do not let jealousy make you stay.

If he loves you true of heart
This could be a brand new start.
If this love he cannot find
Then now is the time to leave him behind.
For love and trust go hand in hand,
Foreign country, foreign land.

Eleanor Lloyd

PICNIC IN THE PARK

The special occasions that arise from events
People gathering, as if invitations had been sent
Arriving with a picnic outside, in the park
With the warm summer sun from morning till dark
Some venues so large, several fields used for days
Gospel and Christian singers, performing on open stage
Country music and dancing, barbecues arranged
Brass bands prepare on their colourful bandstands
Jazz, soul and folk music, people listening enthralled
Symphonic orchestras playing at their festivals
Enjoying the sound of Beethoven and Bach
Sitting with friends till the evening got dark
Tchaikovsky and Vivaldi, Gilbert and Sullivan too
Operatic Arias echoing through
Listening to music of your own choice
Singing in harmony with very good voice
Youngsters enjoying their pop-singing icons
For others, to end. A night at the Proms.

Linda Meadows

THE PATHWAY OF LIFE

We walk along the path of life
Sometimes many roads to choose.
Our burden's getting heavy -
We can hardly move.
Please take this weight from me
For this I cannot bear.
Help me, bright light,
For I know you really care.
Guide me gently as I go
Help me to decide
Which way to walk.
Which path to tread,
My trust in you I bestow.
I cling to you so closely,
I dare not close my eyes.
The crossroads of life are many,
Help me to be *extra* wise.

Gillian Maynard

OUR EARTH

What on Earth is ozone?
What is all the fuss?
What on Earth is climate change?
Is it really down to us?

No more talk of racial hate
And different coloured skin
Are we not just all the same
When you're looking from within?

There really must be no more war
No more graveyard flowers
No more needless loss of life
Let's protect this world of ours.

So let's unite and act right now
To end the pain and sorrow
It really is all down to us
To ensure there is tomorrow.

E M Minter

BETRAYED

You walk into a room, silence, tension, atmosphere,
All I can think of is, *get me out of here!*
We go behind your back, don't know who to believe,
And all along and all this time, I have been deceived.
You all stick together, don't let anybody in,
Frustrated, angry, cross, two-faced, it's a sin.
You make me feel sick, ill, unwell,
There's nothing I can do about it. No way! No how!
You don't believe me, reduced me to tears, I feel I've been betrayed.
You're stubborn and spiteful with the decision which you've made.
Your hatred is spreading like a disease,
I can't take any more, I've been brought to my knees.
It's like the Mafia, *'We will get you out!'*
They'll drag you down, kicking and screaming,
No one will hear you shout.

Melanie May (18)

WINDBACK RACER

In cold metallic spannered form
A two-wheeled hurricane is born
With transferred emerald gleaming frame
Fine balanced poise upholds its fame
Whirring and whirring, gathering speed
Pedalling and puffing and taking the lead
Thrilling with rushes of pollen-filled air
Stinging and smarting and whipping the hair
Unending circles, round and around
Spoke-spiked spinning wheels glancing the ground
Past freeze-frame fields, half a cry
A pocket rocket zooming by
As whooshing down the steep decline
Goes back wind racing, past the line.

Elizabeth Walker

BUT...

How do I choose between love and lust?
Have to make a decision, it's a must
One makes me happy, is safe and secure
The other makes me high, I'm tempted by his allure
He makes me fantasise, drift off to another world
I wish he'd touch me, I wish I was his girl
I imagine what he'd do, the way that he'd kiss
But then I think of all the things I'd miss
Someone who cares, loves me for who I am
If I wasn't in this situation, I'd forever want him as my man
Kind and thoughtful, knows just what to say
Makes sure I know he loves me, day after day
But every time I see the other, I just forget
Something about him, I wish we'd never met
Dream of his touch, his body pressed against me
Running his hands through my hair, how good it would be
But how could I cheat and be unkind?
The situation is out of my hands, no longer in mine
I just hope it turns out right for everyone,
But how can it? Not with what I've just done.

Charlotte Watkins

GETTING OLDER

When you are getting older
Your 'little bits' wear out
You get a touch of stiffening joint,
Or a spot of gout.

Your eyesight seems to fade a bit
Your teeth, they start to rot
You wear an extra cardigan
To keep your body hot.

You go on Saga holidays,
And not the jet-set sort.
Instead of playing football
You find another sport.

You go out to the whist drive
Or a game of bowls you play.
And maybe on a trip by bus
Or the seaside for the day.

I sometimes sit and wonder
Who can these people be?
And then I realise by chance
Oh yes . . . that's Dad and me!

Jenny Wright

FORGOTTEN DREAMS

The endless dream, the silken prose
The restless night and tousled clothes.
The jumbled words and action bright
That steal into the darkest night.
A world of fantasy, so strange
Yet so revealing wind of change.
So on and on until the dawn
When we awaken with a yawn
And although we try with all our might
Forgotten are the secrets of the night.

Jenny Winkworth

UNLIKED

Annoyance, headache, fake,
Lies, deceits you make,
Sifts about supposed sex life,
Bragging usually denotes lack of.

Rudeness seeps from your mind,
Nastiness inflicted; cuts the bind,
Evil looks and snide terms,
Body riddled with cruel worms.

Ugliness just drips out,
Crawling about sucked into somebody else,
Multiplies, never dies,
Just continues to grow inside.

All are consumed; confused,
Taken over been abused,
Hurt, hated and been used,
Sorry you lose.

Your minds have been raped
Suffered the trauma prepared for the fate,
All is needed is to set the date
And wait . . .

Samantha E Whitehouse

A Dollshouse World

I wish I could shrink,
To half scale you see,
I'd live in a dollshouse,
Is where I'd like to be.

In a miniature house,
In a miniature room
By a miniature sink,
Holding a miniature broom.

This world is amazing,
I'd like to be there,
With a miniature comb,
Combing down my miniature hair.

A miniature house,
Would not take long to clean,
With miniature clothes,
In a miniature machine.

A miniature chest
With a miniature drawer,
And a miniature mop,
Cleaning a miniature floor.

Washing a miniature plate,
Or a miniature bath,
It is so very tiny
It all makes me laugh.

A miniature baby,
Still such a charm,
But so very small,
Would slip from your arm.

In the end, so tiny
And always a treasure to keep.

Tracy D Wood

SACRIFICE

Thus this day they gloriously lie
'Pon many a foreign clime,
Portraying-true such valiant hearts
That died in hope - peace to restore
Upon mankind for evermore.
That souls from 'Sceptred Isle'
Shouldst not have sacrificed in vain
Their all, in mortal fear and pain.

Within each far-off battlefield
Brave ones who gave no thought to yield
Lie sleeping now in peace and rest,
Full-well 'tis judged, they didst their best.
Witness now the many who every dying year
Are standing there - in homage bent
At many a place so drear.
Silent, but softly weeping 'tis plain to see,
O'er memories of those who selfless gave
For you and me.

Can it e'er be truly said
That time has come to sad-deny
Our 'precious dead'?
Must thoughts be merely those of 'greater age',
Reflecting-sad that they couldst see
The turning of the final page
Of blessed book of debt still owed by all,
Such cost as ne'er could thus be counted small?

Dennis F Tyc

CARPE DIEM

Had I but world enough and time
to coax each metre, tease each rhyme,
I'd spin a filament so fine
that verses stretched in endless line
and cast their couplets for a chain
around the stars and back again.

But since my skull wears paper-thin,
and every bone requires its pin,
while blood runs cold and thoughts turn sour,
and sands fall faster by the hour,
needs must I snatch what words I can
in all that's left of mortal span.

Peter Watson

THE INTRUDER

Movement across the kitchen floor
The noise abates as they close the door
The owner of the house, now gone
Lots of exploring to be done
Nothing stirs within the house
But wait now, wait, is that a mouse?
From behind a cornflake box appears
A pair of pinky, listening ears
A nose is twitching in the night
Its eyes they search, shining bright
Must be aware, just in case
Don't want to risk or cause a chase
Across the kitchen floor he runs
A valiant effort in search of crumbs
A morsel of cheese or cake will do
A piece of chocolate for him to chew
A chip, a crumb or something nice
A pip, a seed, a grain of rice
Suddenly, a noise rings out
A human coming without a doubt
Don't blow the cover and show he's been
Stay hidden away where he can't be seen
Quickly now, make no mistakes
Make it back to the cornflakes
Faster, faster, up the pace
Doesn't want to show his face

Neil Warren

Fishing Boats

Rouse from the depth of winter's dreams;
wake as sun through the window beams,
rise as the tide on pebbles foam,
watch the gulls as away they roam
to follow trawlers where herring teem,
high on a breeze, their feathers gleam.

Hark at the rigging, creak and groan
as weary now the men come home.
All are glad to see the shore
where each one brings his boat to moor,
tying ropes and spreading nets
to dry in the sun before it sets.

Kathleen Thorpe

MY ANGEL FLEW AWAY

On the day we met, the skies were blue,
I was so happy to be with you,
As time went by we fell in love,
I thanked the heavenly stars above.

We named the day after a while,
And with joy walked down the aisle,
Our folks were there to share our glee,
As we fulfilled our destiny.

The years were good as we were blessed,
With kids who were the very best,
We were so proud as they matured,
To be confident and assured.

Grandchildren came to give us joy,
First a girl and then a boy,
We felt so lucky to have this life,
When other folks had so much strife.

Then one day we said goodbye,
I thought that you could never die,
I opened up my heart to say,
My angel has just flown away.

B Taylor

THE DAY BEGINS

Morning arises stormy and pale
No sun but a very strong gale
Rose petals gather on the grass
And morning dew, which will pass
Then at last the sun came
Ready to burn in colour flame
With all the changes of the day
From early morn to evening rain.

Ann Thompson

THE CRY OF THE EAGLE
(For Caroline)

You touched my heart with your gentle love,
And I heard the eagles cry.
You lifted me above the crowd,
And I felt that I could fly.

Like gentle waves upon the ocean,
Your touch rocked my inner soul,
And weariness and solitude,
Disappeared and I was whole.

Where is love but in the heart,
Where is truth if not within?
And deep within my beating heart
My true love for you did begin.

I felt the brush of your gentle breath,
I saw the beauty buried inside,
And I nurtured you with tender care,
Until our love we couldn't hide.

And I will stand with you my love
Against a world of doubt and scorn,
For I would give my everything
To wake beside you at the dawn.

I ask not much of this earthly life,
Just to hold you close for evermore,
And to hear the eagles cry each day,
Until the cry becomes a roar!

Brian L Porter

THE BLUE TIT

The blue tits make their chattering way,
Along the rambling rose,
Their chattering is no idle talk
They seek their breakfast on each stalk.
Their sparkling wine, a dewdrop clear
Glistening in the sun.
A spider's thread makes them a bed
In which to raise their young.

Valerie Mellor

FLUTTER BY
*(Happy birthdays to my parents with thoughts
of many butterflies in Heaven)*

Orange tip, black and white
Tortoiseshell, her colours so bright
Miraculous metamorphosis
A brief moment of freedom will be his.

A chrysalis clings to a tree -
This life won't last like you or me.
Beautiful Peacock puts up a fight,
His life taken on his first flight.

Crawly caterpillar from egg to grub,
Eating leaves from flower to shrub.
Cabbage white towards extinction
Crops are sprayed for their protection.

Powdery soft wings lightweight
He flies away to find a mate.
Flying low to procreate
Though he'll not know what's in his fate.

Painted lady, flutter by
Gorgeous, fragile, butterfly.
Pity now there are so few
To lighten up my garden hue.

Linda Lawrence

BEAUTIFY THE BUTTERFLY

Strolling endless lane and meadow, through each wooded dell,
Warm sunlight rays over distant vales, the scent of rural smell
The silence of the earthly calm, gave perfect peace 'a sigh . . . !'
When out of nowhere, appeared a moth and then a butterfly.
The quivering of their graceful wings,
Over earth's most precious things
Flowers wild, grass and trees
Like a colourful piece of paper, floating in the breeze!
Not knowing where or when to rest,
These gracious delicate insects; short lived; but do their best,
To dance a wary way and for travellers, he offers a grand display;
Of all the world's most creatures small,
The butterfly; is surely loved best, by all?
He gives us pleasure just to watch and see,
The ways in which he moves and drifts, most blissfully!
Uncaring if a danger lurks along his way,
He may no doubt, survive this day? Who can say!
So little colourful, flamboyant, harmless creature play!
As out of sight you both fade away!
Flutterby: the butterfly, for you I'll pray!
As the colour to our lives you beautifully portray.

William J Lyth

RESTRAINED SECRET

Your soul will be banished, your ashes scattered to the air.
Let the grey eyes of sorrow destroy what you know,
Until your hope and glory are damned with you below.
I hate the weak and despise the ignorant,
I am disrespected; you can escape but not hide.
How far can you run before you realise you're running away,
Fate cannot be stopped, only summoned.
Take off the mask and reveal the three points of illusion,
The five points of power.
There's a blurred line between this world and reality.
Sitting on the outskirts of each, true magic
Cannot be found.

Katy M Lewis

SMILE

Smile that hides
A thousand tears
Turns the tides
No trace of fears

Heart's held tight
To soften the blow
Charts the flight
The ebb, the flow

Time stands still
If you're not here
Swift to fill
When you're so near

Find a strength
From you, so strong
That all makes sense
That we belong

That love is deep
As any sea
A depth to keep
A buoyancy

My pivot, guide me close
To find my feet upon the coast
To reassure that it's okay?
To find my wings and fly away!

Ali Rice

THE SOUND OF YOUR SILENCE

Look at me, look at you
What are you going to do?
The days are here!
The days are gone!
Where's your mind set, is it on?

Eight o'clock in the morning,
Wintertime gives winter's warning.
My tight fist opens,
I'm lost for answers.

The sound of your silence,
Feelings of a different life.
Birds sky-dive between city buildings
One hour passes, winter's sky darkens
This day
Sounds of your silence
Won't go away.

Andrew Ryan

ON A LAZY SUMMER'S DAY

I'm so relaxed I could lay here for hours,
Watching buzzing bees on the flowers.

I take a sip of ice cold beer,
Not a voice for miles, just sweet birdsong
That's all I can hear.

I look up at a wonderful clear blue sky,
It's times like this I wish I could fly.

Butterflies with wings of many colours
All around me,
It's summer days like this we all love to see.

As the sun beams down on me,
I can't think of anywhere else I'd rather be.

Jeff Slominski

You

I think of you all the time.
You're always on my mind,
Why won't you be mine?
I see you in my dreams,
I think about you all the time.
So stupid to me it seems.
Why won't you be mine?
I know I saw it coming,
Or at least I claim to have,
For this is the last and final thing
I do,
For this, it's just for you.

Sophie Peppercorn (13)

NATURE LOVING BOY

Lace, May and butterfly early took my eye
Moths too and dragonfly did I joyfully espy
Woodlice to me not nice,
Ants, of these I be no sychoplant.
Birds of the feathered kind, please my mind
Buzz of the bee is honey to me,
Wish it were part of dawn symphony.
Caressing mine ears enchantingly,
Rousing a drowsy me
In manner velvety

Seek a place in the sun,
Time out for a little fun,
Along pool-sides, canal and riverbanks run.
At fishing, take a crack
Wended my way home
With jam-jar containing, retaining
Wee red-finned roach,
And ragged, fin stickleback.
Netted easily in pea-bag stockingnet
Hearth throbbing like a lute,
On sighting minuscule dinosaur
Strangest thing, I ever saw
A newt, really cute.
Matched by black, flagellating jelly blob,
Prelude to a frog.
Should there be showers,
Seek shelter in flower bowers,
Primroses and bluebells in season
Appealing to man and boy's reason,
So happy to discover, they be a nature lover.

Graham Watkins

NOBODY

All alone I stand and stare
Into nothing
At nothing
I am nothing
A nobody.
Well that's what someone told me!
Someone that was a somebody!
How do you become a somebody?
If people like you, are you a somebody
If people love you?
If you do something perhaps.
If something makes you a somebody,
Then nothing should make you a nobody!
And as you can't make anything out of nothing -
So nobody is a nobody?
Apart from me of course
'Cause I was told I was . . .
By a somebody
So that makes me one of a kind
So you can have your somebody's
And I'll be a nobody
So I will stand here all alone
And stare at you all
Into nothing.
At nothing.
Having fun?

Nadine Dudley

THE ALTERNATIVE DRIVING TEST

When you go to supermarkets -
Safeway, Tesco and the rest -
There is a thought that you should take
The shopping trolley driving test.

The designer of these trolleys
Was a great genius, you know;
Because wherever they are pushed,
It's somewhere else they go.

These wibbly-wobbly monsters
Have a mind that's all their own;
So if you cannot pass this test,
Use a basket - or stay home!

Roger Williams

FATED FLIGHT

Our agendas were different,
We were both in a hurry,
You crossed my path,
In the day's dawning flurry.
Were you too fast,
Or me too slow?
Could I have stopped?
No, I don't think so!
But I heard the thud
And the final flutter,
As you fell to the ground
Rest stop, the gutter.
I guess you don't know
How much I regret,
The final collision,
When we both met.
So I give you my thoughts,
This man with machine
I didn't want to hurt you,
I'm really not mean.

Sue Umanski

CITIZEN'S UNITE

I would like to live in a peaceful world
where friendliness prevails
And where society isn't bothered much
with those crimes that fill up jails

The ordinary folk can create this
if they wish a decent life
But they have to work together
to banish wars and strife

They have an overall majority
so they should win with ease
To curb those politicians
who use them as they please

Wars should not be needed
when countries can't agree
There should be skilful negotiations
with no place for insanity

We have had plenty of experience now
to show that war is no solution
With the blood shown on the poppy fields
through those mad political institutions

Lachlan Taylor

PUNCH-DRUNK

One
Blood on the sand, and Mr Punch
Is still boxing Judy's head . . .
It's that old seaside magic:

Carousels of laughter,
Ice creamed lips
And a smack across the poll.

You see, the trick is easy . . .
Just a simple play on words:
'Now that's the way to do it!'

And so he does.

Two
Mr Punch has taken centre stage again.
this time he has a wooden-club concealed
beneath his sleeve. Look! There by his
wrist's unbuttoned cuff, you can see
the stained grain shining through. Takes a bow.

Judy is in the wings, waiting; her white face
hidden by her porcelain fingers. He calls
to one side: 'Judy, is that you?' Steals the show
and we all applaud. Then silence. You can
almost feel those curtains trembling.

Louis Foley

Two Candles In The Window

I put candles in my window every single night,
And the flames that burn so brightly are my parents guiding light,
For I know that somewhere out there, in Heaven up above,
They know that I think about them for they shower me with love.

When I look into the mirror, the reflection that I see
Is my mother and my father looking right back out at me.
For I have my father's hair and eyes, my mother's lovely face,
And no one else that walks this Earth could ever take their place.

They are my morning sunshine, the moon that lights my night,
The brightest star that's shining that guides me through my life.
I will always be proud of them and what they did for me,
So I place two candles in the window that I know they both will see.

Now I watch the candles flicker as they slowly dim and die,
My heart is filled with sadness and teardrops fill my eyes,
But when the day is over and night-time comes again,
I will place my candles in the window and think once more of them.

They are always there beside me in the things I say and do,
Their love and happy memories will last me my life through,
One day I know we'll meet again, though I know not where or when,
So I'll put my candles in the window to show I think of them.

They are but tiny little flames, but the flames of love burn bright,
And I hope they both can see them in the darkness of the night,
Then when my life is over, all the love they gave to me,
Will be passed on to my children, so that they may light candles for me.

Kathleen Christine Bennett

THIS IS ME

I thought I knew who I was
Sometimes I catch glimpses of who I could have become
I wonder what if, what could have been and what is now
So I open my window to the world and beckon it in
I give into the fear and embrace the unknown
I drown in a sea of hope and uncertainty
I open my heart to you - *this is me.*

Sheena Harris

WILL YOU BE MINE?

I will love you forever
I want you forever
Since I met you we're going places
We've never been before
I wanna see you all of the time
I wanna hold you until the end of time
My heart is beating like a drum
I wanna hold your hand and look into your eyes
I wanna see you smile and most of all babe
Will you be mine until the end of time?

Geoff Beatty

SOLDIERS OF FREEDOM

From the time immemorial, came the greatest song,
That the soldier is like a diamond, or even the hardest stone.
We don't fight to be heroes, only do what we can
For the honour of our country, for the honour of our land.
Because we are people of freedom, who are born to a free land,
And for this we always fight and for this we always stand.
If somebody ever mentions our names and what we've done,
There have been many before us and there'll be many as time is gone
We don't have to do much, just a duty of right minds,
For our lives, land and freedom, we will put up the greatest fight.
Because we are people of freedom, who are born to a free land,
And for this we always fight and for this we always stand.

Kevin Kondol

SILENCE IS NOT GOLDEN

Silence is not golden
When the bee's about to sting
The rats are in the rafters
And birds are on the wing
A lump of mud surrounds them
And makes one want to scream.
Rotten is the posy
Fermenting in the bin.

Marilyn Jones

PARADISE

What's your aim in life? What do you desire most?
In a troubled world of wars, sickness and pain,
There doesn't seem much to achieve,
Sometimes you think you have won through
Only to lose it all as suddenly as it came.
Don't despair my friend, I see a glow of light,
And it's getting brighter and closer every day.
A radiance will cover this land.
Jesus, Our King is coming to reign over a new world.
The radiance will show on our faces,
Our King will bring healing and peace,
We thought we could never obtain,
And our King promises all this will last forever.

Margaret Waudby

THE DEAL

Lord I want to make a deal
I'm broke and times are hard.
I will promise not to steal
if you clear my credit card.

I didn't steal, I didn't thieve.
You did nothing, that's a fact.
But Lord I truly do believe
so, can we make another pact?

Age Concern needs volunteers
and my driving isn't the best.
So if I help a few old dears
will you see I pass my test?

I was convinced I'd pass in style
but I never got that far.
I'd only driven half a mile
when you let me crash the car!

We're three nil down in the FA Cup.
Please restore some parity.
If you'll just trip their keeper up
I'll give five pounds to charity.

Minutes to go, the scores the same,
I may as well get my coat.
We're sure to lose this vital game
so I'll keep my five-pound note!

I don't like wigs, they're just not cool.
So although I don't feel 'called',
if I go off to Bible School
will you stop me going bald?

You've really made me look a fool.
It simply isn't fair.
I enrolled at Bible School
but you still took all my hair.

I thought we could agree a deal?
I thought you couldn't lie?
Confused; I didn't know what to feel
so I shouted at the sky.

'My Lord, as far as I can see
You never keep your word.'
Then Jesus softly spoke to me
and this is what I heard.

'I only made one promise to you
on a cross, long, long ago.
That I would be your Saviour,
the friend you've come to know.
I've given you a gift of life,
my child don't complain or moan.
One day you may face *real* strife
but you will *never* be alone.'

Gavin Capstick

CLOUDS

When I glance at the sky,
What do I see?
A lot of fluffy clouds
Creating pictures for me.

I can see faces,
Sometimes angels too.
With their outspread wings,
It's really quite a view.

Sometimes I see black clouds,
Hovering in the sky.
They are like monsters staring,
From way up high.

The clouds that I see,
Do not stand still for long,
They move around, so very fast,
Till my pictures have gone.

Doreen E Hampshire

LIFELONG LOVE

I gaze at her lovingly, as she sits on the chair
Longing to be with that girl over there
I just can't resist her, I can't help but show it
She's way in control, and doesn't she know it

A flirtatious seductress, she'll tease me all day
Sending her aura and calling my way
Her body so perfect, so slender and white
She's delicate, gentle, a beautiful sight

She's been with me for years and she's honest and true
She's calming, supportive and carries me through
Still I yearn for her touch since our very first kiss
There's no other woman I've wanted like this

But my family are worried, they say she's no good
They say I must leave her, if only I could
She's the kind of lady I've desired all along
How can love like this be wrong?

But sadly this love affair must come to an end
I'm losing my lady and very best friend
But before she must leave me, just a few more drags
This time I'm determined, to give up these fags.

Lesley Heath

KIRKWOOD HOSPICE

Peace has settled here.
It is all embracing
It rests in the quiet garden
Flows in at open doors
Shines through the windows.

Noise does not intrude.
The whirring of a fan
The murmur of voices
Add only a sense of calm.

Here time is a friend.
Those who rest awhile
Are given leave with love
To say goodbye, as gently
They pass into that goodnight.

Brenda Brown

THE ILLEGAL IMMIGRANTS' PHRASE-BOOK

If you are brought to England without approval
and live in dread of a swift removal,
if you plan to escape eviction
you must speak the language with conviction.

There's no need to study at college
and burden your brain with a vast knowledge.
Here's cost effective, sound advice
just a few key phrases will suffice.

There's no call to tax your imagination
there's stock phrases to suit any situation.
In no time you'll be so elated
because you'll speak English like a native.

What's the problem? Can I help you? Have a nice day.
That is all you'll need to say.
If you approve, it's fab, it's great.
If you're angry, just watch it mate!

How do you do? I haven't a clue.
Cheers. I'll have a pint, same for you?
What's on telly? Where's the lolly?
A woman's a slapper or a dolly.

Drop dead, get lost, get stuffed
no one now can call your bluff.
It's rip-off, that's cool and stuff.
This selection will prove enough.

Now your identity will be protected
you will never even be suspected.
Fair enough matey get it sorted
speak thus - you'll never get deported.

John B Morris

UNTITLED

You've cried upon my shoulder
I've kissed your tears away
I've watched you sleeping at night
Held your hand throughout the day

I've shared your tender hugs
Felt the warmth of your embrace
Seen the sparkle in your eyes
And the gleam upon your face

I've felt the hurt and pain
Of whenever we're apart
And sometimes you have cried
When there's sorrow in your heart

At times it may have seemed
That there's nothing left to gain
And once or twice you've wondered
If you'll ever ease the pain

Whenever you feel this way
And I know sometimes you do
Please try to remember
How much that I love you.

G Quinney

THE RETURN OF THE LAST OF THE MOHICANS

In the early years of the twentieth century, a strange story was heard in the lands that adjoined the Mississippi river.

The tale concerned an incident, reputedly true, in which a young farmer came face-to-face with the ghost of an Indian chief, who he thought to be the son of another great chief, Geronimo.

The farmer, whose name cannot be recalled, was so surprised that he is believed to have suffered a heart seizure from which he never recovered.

The moral of this story is -

Do not believe in ghosts, as worry might bring on anxiety, leading to an early grave.

Brian M Wood

GETTING OLD

People say I'm getting old
The truth I say is to be told
My life I've lived for sixty years
This life of mine with you I share

When I was born there reigned a king
Now he's passed by, we have a queen
So young they say, she takes his place
To rule the land, she has to face

I grew up and I did share
This love of mine with you my dear
We raised a family of our own
And they grew up, to raise their own

My looks are changing as I grow old
My once black hair has turned to gold
This frame of mine that once was strong
Is weak and frail and takes its toll

So as the years have just passed by
I still look up to see the sky
I still have a life to live and share
With all of you, I hold so dear.

R Claxton

WELCOME BACK

Sitting in your armchair,
Do you ever get out of there,
Looking at you now, it's so sad,
Where is the mother-in-law I once had?
Full of gloom,
In your sitting room,
No conversation, watching TV,
You are quite oblivious to your son and me.

Seeing you so frail,
How could we fail,
To feel sad for you,
When you used to be so active too,
Suddenly you start to chat,
Well what do you think of that,
You give us both a cheeky smile,
You were there all the while,
I have seen that smile before,
Welcome back, mother-in-law.

Maureen Arnold

MILESTONES OF MARRIAGE

We leave behind those urgent days of youth,
For magic indefinable, a sudden joyful truth.
A wish to share the passing years with husband or with wife,
To face the tribulations of what we know as life.
Pleasures of a new-made garden in the early morn,
Souls uplifted at the sight of our dear first-born.
The pulling on the heart strings when the children leave the nest,
Sadness in the family when a loved one's laid to rest.
Holidays and Christmas, all those bright New Years,
Laughter with grandparents who often hide their tears.
Milestones of marriage, of our life and of our love,
All those golden moments blessed by God above.

June Picken

My Love

The morning bird's song swiftly rose,
As gentle as the soft wind blows,
And autumn leaves that turn to brown,
When slowly as I lay you down,
A kiss from your sweet lips you give,
To raise my spirits and life to live,
Your love it means the world to me,
With eyes that sparkle as you see,
My love is yours for evermore,
My dreams, my heart, my soul, all yours.

Mel Price

I'M GOING ON ME HOLIDEES!

Once a year we have a well earned break,
They call it a holiday, two weeks we take.

All the different places, where there is lots of sunshine
Decided to go to Spain, all-inclusive that's just fine.

Ticking off the calendar, crossing off all the dates,
Packing all the suitcases, saying ta-ra to your mates.

Finding the journey long and a bit of a pain,
Going early to the airport, to get that all important plane.

Free drinks at the bar, restaurant full of lovely food,
Couldn't refuse any of it, that would be rude!

Before the holiday it was *Weight Watchers* then down to the gym,
Doing extra exercise to make yourself thin.

Weighing in by the week, watching calories by the score,
Then all the weight gets piled on and shorts don't fit anymore.

Lying on the beach, got a sun bed from the man,
Putting all the lotions on, to get an all over tan.

It's hard going on your hols, I think you will agree,
All the things you have to do, for just two weeks by the sea.

So when your holidays are over and you haven't a damn thing to wear,
It's home to start that *bloody* diet, to get thin again for next year.

Barbara Jackson

WARLORD

The warlord of Atlantis
'Tis he who rules the sea
His trident raised in anger
'Tis he to challenge thee
His realm the deepest kingdom
His home the ocean floor
Those ghostly wrecks an epitaph
Of ships that sail no more
Those rusting chains and anchors
And cannons by the score
The spoils of many battles
Were fought away off shore
Lie treasures in abandon
Of silver, gold and plate
The Spanish Maine and piracy
Of ships that met their fate
The lives of many seamen
To count a thousand score
Their graves the ocean bottom
They disobeyed the warlord's law.

A Sheard

THAT'S MY BOY

He wears the uniform of modish youth,
A baseball cap (reversed) upon his head:
His T-shirt message, blatantly uncouth,
Displayed from neck to knee in lettered spread.
And out-size jeans as wide as they are long
Sweep ragged trails behind his Reebok'd feet,
While in his head-phoned ears this week's pop song
Dictates a pace, now moody, now upbeat.

Skateboard in hand, all dusty from his ride,
Drawn home by hunger and computer game
He quickens his ungainly teenage stride:
And though it's late he's not the one to blame.
But even when he slouches on his chair
In posture calculated to annoy,
I can't deny maternal pride is there,
For *warts and all* I'll own him. That's *my* boy!

Janet L Smith

QUID

Pollution in the sky,
                air and light.
Noise on the road,
                car and bike.

Too much haste,
                run and speed.
Too much waste,
                water and feed.

Lots of greed,
                money and power.
Want, want, want,
                makes me cower.

          Neglecting our families,
          Subjecting our kids,
          Regretting our mistakes,
          All for a quid.

          This world is a money spinner
          covered in a web,
          But some places have a hole in it
          and will end up dead!

Sally Cocking

What Is?

What is red? A rose is red
Lying on the comfy bed.

What is pink? Skin is pink
As smooth as mine, don't you think?

What is yellow? Daffodils are yellow
Growing in the meadow.

What is black? My gran's cat is black
Sleeping on an anorak.

What is purple? Flowers are purple
Growing in a circle.

What is white? Clouds are white
Covering the sun that shines so bright.

Katie Elizabeth Shaw (9)

AGE

Children playing hand in hand,
People jogging on the sand,
Grannies tripping, oh what fun!
Look, there goes another one!

The wrinkles on an old man's face,
Droop and dangle, pace by pace,
The skinny skeleton's creaking limbs
Shows a sign of all his sins.

The walking stick shakes in his hand,
His ageing leg is wrapped in band.
When time overtakes him, the old man fades,
He slowly dies and deteriorates.
He shrinks and shrivels into a lump,
And then drops into a grave with a very loud thump!

Gordon Ming-Li Ho

TRANQUILLITY

Stars burst in a deep black sky, making the heavens dance,
alive with diamond light.
You touch my face and bluebells ring their happy song
You are the one I have waited for - for so long
I explode at the smallest of things.
You just say, 'Hush!' and take me under your wings.
I am the flame, but you are the fire.
Who is to say has the greatest desire?
I look into your eyes and see the beauty of tranquillity.

Jacky Stevens

THE TRAVELLER

Though I choose not to dwell in a home,
I carry my thoughts wherever I roam,
Seeking friendship and kindred spirits
To talk about life as I pass by earth's limits.

There was someone I loved long ago,
She married for wealth and left me low.
So now I stick to my faithful old bitch,
She won't desert me or give me the slip.

I've a way with horses, dogs and birds,
Although originally from modest birth,
Slept in orchards, fields and ditches,
Far from the cities' magnificent riches.

I've work in circuses and fairs,
In farmyards when jobs were scarce.
Been in stables grooming horses -
Had to live by my wits and resources.

They say I'm green-fingered, my plants
Seem to grow - vegetables ripen when I sow.
Fruits lie mellow and choice in my hand,
Suppose I'm deeply attached to the land.

Can write a poem, play the guitar;
Have slept with gypsies under the stars.
Had a stall in markets, selling wares,
I've a taste for girls with long dark hair.

I enjoy a pint and often a dram,
Especially when it's Yuletide again.
But when I lie down to my final rest,
It's enough to know I've done my best.

Christine Stallion

UNTITLED 2003

Flashing back through the years
Hopes dashed, yet more tears
The Reaper harvests ingrown fears
Lain down, by misuse of throttle and gears

Raking over coals gone cold
Shining knights, once so bold
Their history once foretold
By a Soothsayer, so old, for a coin of gold

Miffed by confusion, caught in a loop
Strangled by the hangman's noose
Drawn and quartered, thrown from the poop
Frightened chickens, a fox amongst their coop

Striving, branching, onward and out
Taking root, mighty oak, from an acorn you sprout
A nipper's lip, heavy with pout
Until spawning is over, man is left only with doubt

Each step in time causes a ripple
So often, downed tools, leaves the all-important ungreased nipple
Relentlessly, this world grinds on,
Leaving space drowned in its favourite tipple
Only our ashes remain, the future's trophies, of the pasts destitute
Now forever immobile.

Lynne O'Connor

DREAMS

At nine o'clock I go to bed
I'm always glad to rest my head
The day was long and soon I will be
Asleep to dream and dreams are free

Once I dreamt that I was king
I had to wear a diamond ring
I ruled my people in my land
The ring was bright upon my hand

One day I lost my diamond ring
No longer then could I be king
I woke up with a start to find
My finger in the window blind

Another time I was a sailor
At this I was a dismal failure
I couldn't stand up on the ship
My feet just would not get a grip.

Some nights I'm glad when I wake up
On others I'm quite sad
For once I won The FA Cup
Presented by my dad.

Muriel Purdy

TRUE INTENT

In dappled light of forest glen
Lightly did I tread and stealthy on moss and leaf
Pressed with eagerness and expectation did I creep.
Failure was my dread
The aim at what lay ahead
My doubts no less
Disappointment or frustration my problem to address
Error misjudgement a drastic mess
Oh to have that power
Wishing to open opportunity's door
Control the hands of time and fate
To see again that sight
As seen so many times before with sheer delight.
So lightly did I tread
Onward now with heavier heart
Though failure was my fear, sadness prevailed
My mind was clear.
That sight again so steel my will
Breath held body still
One shot and moments pass
Bright blood spread to stain the mossy grass.
That aged monarch lay in death to stately die
Tear in my eye
No more to lightly tread himself with head held high
Flared nostrils to the sky.
Those battling days before, that lusty roar
To chase with intent as nature meant
Now to rut no more
What a stag - ailing, failing, part of the cull.

Ron Powell

TECHNOLOGY

You sit there almost quiet, indifferent to my plight
If you were human I'm positive, we'd end up in a fight
You're supposed to ease my workload, not make it last a day
If you have one more fatal error, you're really going to pay.

The software's loaded perfect, but you just spit it out
Then you simply freeze up and watch me scream and shout
Give you the keyboard death grip, of control alt delete
Once again the boot-up sequence, you slowly now repeat.

Come on you better show me, the desktop I had before
Otherwise I'll grab you, and throw you out the door
It's now gone into scan disk, checking for an error
My heartbeat's mad, my hands are gripped, you have me full of terror.

The screen goes black, the hard disk whirrs, I hear the magic sound
The shortcuts, toolbars, reappear against a blue background.
I'm happy now; you're working fine, until another day
When things go wrong, you get me vexed and my temper starts to fray.

Michael Clenton

SOLILOQUY OF A DOOMED QUEEN

Fate's thread rescinded on the loom,
Each tangled skein considered well
As I ponder in my darkening room,
In solitude, where shadows dwell

Of old within my sentinel tower,
Which I vainly strove to fortify
Against royal whim and cardinal's power,
With every stone, another lie.

All the bright and golden gifts,
Lucratively reap'd in stealth
Through the sieve of life it sifts
This miser's hope - but not of wealth.

A lowly state we must endure,
Impoverished hours of strife and pain
Reject I would this state impure.
Alas, the moon must wax and wane.

O turn the hourglass, I implore,
To sentient days I once held dear
And summer smiles that are no more,
But banished ghosts of yesteryear.

Across the mirror of my mind
This spectral host flits to and fro
On contemplation do I find,
Mere shadow play in a shadow show

Couched with my slender form,
Opium'd night - spawned dreams prevail
'Neath slumberous depths an inner storm
What searing passions thus assail.

Nightly doth she softly burn,
Behold the naked moon on high
Her celestial secrets would I learn
Of realms where even death must die.

Cold, so cold this chamber wall,
Be done! No succour tears can bring
The sky shall be my funeral pall,
And the ravenous worm, my husband king.

Joseph Cope

WHEN ARE YOU COMING TO BED?

On the eve of Village Flower Show every window is alight;
There's much cursing and much crying for tonight's the longest night.

Section I is madly digging 'neath a fitful August moon:
Five potatoes (one variety) are needed very soon;
Five runner beans, three beetroots, five courgettes, the ninth shallot
Must all be found and measured and displayed without a spot.

Section II is armed with secateurs and hunting floribunda:
The wind of change blew yesterday and now there's talk of thunder.
The tuberous begonia is looking rather frail
And yesterday's nasturtiums were superb - before the gale.

Section III has gone ballistic and is cooking for its life:
There's a gingerbreaded husband and a marmaladed wife
And a birthday cake in pieces and a tin of blackened bread
And the cat has had the pastry and been sick upon the bed.

Section IV is running riot. It's Red Indians this year!
So the kitchen's full of feathers (and some naked hens, I fear).
While his parents climb the Totem Pole, both longing for a whisky,
Their son designs a poster claiming 'Alcohol is risky'.

Section V is thumbing wildly through a hundred glossy prints
To find that photo of 'My Pet' - without the orange tints;
The heaviest vegetable marrow has been ringed with booby traps
And the home-made garden ornament is safely under wraps.

And thus we leave them, hopeful of the morrow's sure success.
Is the Village Flower Show worth it? A resounding, heartfelt . . .

Jane Clarke

WALKING

A whole life spent walking
Walking on the wrong side of the road
A lifetime of missed opportunities
Little chance to lighten the load.

Walking amongst the ignorant
Always misunderstood
Walking amongst the blind
The self righteous and the good

Walking amongst the eluded
Those who profess to know much more
And the guardians by proxy
Who bar opportunity's door

Walking amongst the senseless
The wise man and the fool
Walking amongst the bleeding hearts
The inept, inane and the cruel

Walking amongst the aimless
The ambitious and the strong
Walking amongst minds so weak
They know not right from wrong

Walking with futility
In an attempt to spread the word
Walking toward eternity
Never to be heard.

Paul F Clayton

Patio Panic

I spent the weekend pottering
With rubs and pots for hours.
The geraniums are still in bed
And the fuchsias lost their flowers.

We went away on holiday
And pests, bugs, slugs and snails
Moved in and had a lovely time,
Along with rain and gales.

The judges will be coming soon,
There's no time for delay
For the pots and tubs I've chosen
To be ready for display.

I thought that I had so much time,
But now the day is here.
Then I had a phone call,
It's been cancelled 'til next year.

Janet Fludder

LONELY AND CONFUSED

A story starts, a story ends
I feel lonely like I have no friends
With my heart on my sleeve I hope it mends
I'm not as strong as I like to think I am
So I pretend . . .
I'm still just a boy forced to be a man
I'm confused, don't know how to cope
But I do what I can
And there's no escape not even when I dream
As my tears still stream
Peer pressure can sting
With all the confusion it will bring
So I say to you, 'Take it from my point of view
Walk a mile in my shoes and see what you can do!'
To make things better, I'll never let ya
Put me down
Never let you see me frown.
I've had a look around, in my life I mean
And it's the things I've seen make me realise
How stupid I have been
I know if I'm to see things through,
I'll have to be stronger
But the way I feel now I just hope
I won't live much longer.
                        I'm sorry!

M A Beckett

THE GRAND JUMBLE SALE

The attic is full. The shed door won't shut,
And the garage has no more room to put
Any more items that we have amassed.
With nowhere to put things, I'm feeling harassed!

The doors are shut tight. The stalls are all laid,
Piled high with goods, some new, some frayed.
From coats, vests, gloves and hats,
To lamps, pans, bags and mats.

There's all sorts of things, some good, some not!
Something for all, be it chair or cot.
What is classed as someone's folly, is another's treasure,
Perhaps giving someone a lot of pleasure.

Queues are now growing beyond the door.
Can't keep them waiting any more.
So open the floodgates and let them in,
Our grand jumble sale is now in full swing.

Patricia Burgess

TOTS TO TEENS

From Barbie dolls and cuddly toys
To make-up, sleepovers and chasing boys
From football, fishing and making rude noises
To gym, keeping fit and broken voices.

Growing up fast, the years flying by
School soon over and college draws nigh
These are the years they begin to grow
Finding their way, ready to go.

University beckons for some, not all
The pace is fast and some will fall
At the first hurdle they lose the race
We will be there to save their face.

Look forward my child, onwards not back
We will be there to keep you on track
To guide you and help you to find your place
In a future secured at your very own pace.

Be diligent, work hard and try your best
You will succeed, you won't be suppressed
Try, try and try again
Think of all you'll achieve, it won't be in vain.

Jacqui Beddow

WHISPERS

Do you hear the whispers rustling in a room,
those partly shadowed messages, soft secrets in a womb?
Can you spot the twinkle or the tear in someone's eye,
the rising blush upon a cheek, the reason for a sigh?
Wonder at a cryptic smile, veiled by fluttering hands,
floating like a mirage in the heat of desert sands?

Do you ever hurt inside with another person's pain,
feel their bitter anguish, drenched in icy rain?
Can you share the agony of a bleeding broken heart,
repair the jagged pieces of those fate pulled apart?
Provide an arm to lean on, be a shelter from the cold,
an unexpected friendship, something warm to hold?

Do you listen to your doubts in the lonely hours of night,
asking awkward questions as to wrong or right?
Can you hope to justify the things that you have done,
why you chose to stay and fight or why you chose to run?
Are you such an innocent, white as virgin snow,
or do the stains need washing, do you think they show?

Do you wink at passers-by as you walk along life's path,
be the cause of happiness, the one that makes them laugh?
Can you destroy their devils with the arrows of soft smiles,
while travelling on to destiny for your allotted miles?
The source of wondrous legends to fill your children's dreams,
a knight upon a unicorn that gallops to their screams.

Jim Barnette

BELLYBUTTONS

'What are bellybuttons for?'
I asked my dad when I was small.
He replied that they were there, that's all,
And were there for no real need at all.

So one day, whilst in the bath,
With plastic boat and squeaky duck,
Towards my tummy did I look,
And then I knew - how I did laugh!

Bellybuttons are where they are, you see,
To tell you where your belly must be.
And if your tum does shiver and shake,
You'll know where you have tummy ache!

Paul Reynard

THE REVERED PINT

Tradition is created by repetitious behaviour of culture patterns
over the years
And one important example for Britons has been
the consumption of its beers
We have made merry for centuries in taverns and inns
And from an alcoholic haze enjoyed many pleasantries
and even a few sins.
Tales of woe, intrigue, roistering and wenching
have been captured by many writers,
Often with the sole intent of telling a story to delight us.
Whatever the brew, distilled, beer, ale and mead
They have all fulfilled an essential need.
A pint to celebrate any event, important or otherwise
Is an automatic response and is no surprise.
It plays an integral part of our social behaviour
And its consumption is oft regarded as a problem saviour.
But it's the pint we relish and not that foreign lager,
For the British the pint is part of their historical saga.

Allen Jessop

THE TEARS

I see a tear upon your face
    As fine and so fragrant like delicate lace
Your eyes so tender glisten there
    Reflecting light in your shining hair.
I wonder now as I see you here
    What pain, what words had made those tears

So warm, so real to mar that cheek
    I long to kiss, that smile to seek.
I see that tear quite often now
    And long to comfort you somehow
To take away those thoughts that pain

To bring you sunshine from the rain
    To give you love and tender care
To hold your hand, to touch your hair.
    Now dry your eyes and smile again
Your love will triumph over pain.

E F Croker

EMOTIONS

A wide-eyed baby's smiling face
Unaware of life's rat-race
So innocent, just so content
Those times, it seems, just came and went

A racing heart, a dreamy mind
With thoughts of love - so hard to find
Emotions flying high then low
The sad times which pass by so slow

Such happy times you wished would stay
When suddenly they're 'snatched' away
Sorrow, anger, desolation
Dreaded thoughts of deprivation

Reminiscing, deep in thought
The years went fast, they seemed too short
Once contemplating times ahead
Now living for each day instead . . .

Della McGowan

A TEAR I CRIED

The sky is dark, almost black
The drizzle is steady
The air fresh,
I stand silent, deep in thought
Thinking, thinking.

A tear runs down my face
As I recall past events
Some have been sad,
They cannot be forgotten
Cannot be forced from my memory
Reflections from my life.

Living as I am today
Is of little importance,
I am tormented by my own failure
My past.
Dreams have not been fulfilled
And never will be now,
Such is life.
So much sorrow
So much unsaid or undone.

The drizzle continues
As if it knew
What my tears were for
The dark night is like my heart
Silent and alone.

George S Johnstone

FISHY FORECASTS EARLY 2003

Michael Fish said,
'Snow in the south east
But in the south west at least
It will be dry and bright.'
Yet in Devon, all around us was white
Due to heavy snowfall!

I rang to say, 'Here in Devon
It's snowing thick and fast.'
But in his next broadcast,
Michael Fish said, 'Snow in the south east,
But in the south west at least
It will be dry and bright.'
That despite all around being white
Due to heavy snowfall.
Does he work for the Department of Misinformation?

Catherine Blackett

THE VAMPIRE

Appear after dark, the vampire at night,
To quench its thirst, ready to bite.
A fine bloody snack you will make,
To stand any chance, a mallet and stake.

The vampire moves closer, you're frozen with fear,
The smell of death as she draws near
Mystically enchanting, a beautiful face,
Drifting still nearer with elegance and grace.

Ivory-white fangs that gleam in the dark,
Piercing your flesh, so painfully sharp.
Strangely, a feeling of peace held tight in her arms,
Your once unwilling mind now turning to calm.

She's satisfied her thirst, you fall to the ground,
In a second she's gone, no whisper of sound.
Death has not happened as you thought it would do,
But you're not dead, immortal now, a creature of the night too.

No more day-walking, you stay out of the sun,
Waiting for the end of eternity that will never come.
Appear after dark, the vampire at night,
Waiting for mortals that smell good enough to bite.

Deborah McDowall

The Postman

Who will not deny the exciting day
When the postman comes your way,
Sometimes it's just junk mail,
Or letters caught in a big sale.

Parcels and boxes rarely arrive,
Unless one really does strive,
Leaflets and parcels litter each day,
Makes one keener for being away.

Bank holidays ruin the post,
Always cause problems for most,
Seems a special letter is delayed
For reasons not always explained.

Thought the PO strikes are few,
No one ever gets in a stew,
Who would like to be up at four,
Just to call with mail at your door?

Birthdays, announcements, bills arrive,
But without all these we would survive,
Some things we miss in days of bliss,
Surely we cannot give postie a miss . . .

Bill Burkitt

BLOOD TIES

Blood is thicker than water,
but those ties can falter.
It's a human goldfish bowl,
pain inflicts their collective soul.

Someone puts a foot wrong,
the fall-out lasts all too long.
The fumes pollute their hearts,
forgiveness is harder to reach.

One unit and the same pain,
pride and the selfish leave a stain.
The only way out's going in,
inside their hearts they can win.

Bitterness and anger,
so far it's been saved,
but life's too short,
to take it to the grave.

Anthony Welsh

FUTURE

I'm sat at a crossroads,
Pondering what should I do,
Whilst people keep telling me,
'It's all up to you.'

I've no sense of direction,
I've no indication of what I want to be,
I'll have to wait to find out
What the future has in store for me.

I'm fed up, bored and broke,
If I eat another jam sandwich, I think I'll surely choke.
All my letters I receive are red,
I have very little inspiration to get out of bed.

I'm not looking for millions,
Just enough to get by.
It's not that I'm lazy,
Because I do forever try.

Some days are better than others I guess,
But it does not excuse the fact that I'm still in a terrible mess.

S A Almond

SHAP ABBEY

Golden dawn spans the lightless dome,
Wrapping night in pink-fingered clasp,
Veiling life with the Midas touch
To hold history in its timeless grasp.

Shadowed by the abbey's height,
A newborn lamb begins to bleat,
Looks from behind a comforting ewe
To where golden image and blue sky meet.

Stones that howl as the wind rushes by,
Birds that wheel round the broken grace,
Lifting to God in prayers and chants
Crescendo-ing from the rocky base.

Water's cloth unfurls and glides,
Rippling about the abbey's seat.
The Lowther sweeps over gleaming stones,
Trodden smooth by ancient feet.

Pause at the foot of the reaching tower,
Head thrown back in wondrous gaze
At a piece of sky with crumbling frame;
Heavenward eyes with brimming praise.

Katie Hale

POWER

Power is something that many people seek.
Power is something they think they could enjoy,
So they can overcome the mighty or subjugate the weak.
But power which is used wrongly can become sin's alloy.

Power can be a source of good or evil,
It can be used wisely or alternatively abused.
If we have it we should exercise it with caution,
To ensure that our authority is not misused.

It is said that power corrupts and that absolute power corrupts absolutely,
Down the ages despots and dictators have proved this to be true,
Adolph Hitler and Rasputin are two good examples,
Their history shows the damage misuse of power can do.

On the other hand the pages of history will reveal
The names of people who obtained power and used it well,
In their efforts to promote peace and understanding,
For the benefit of all the nations who on Earth do dwell.

Power is something which is given to us in trust,
In the hope that it will be well used,
This is a responsibility that we must accept,
For to use it wrongly can never be excused.

Ron Martin

PLEASE STOP!

If I wait here long enough will the shouting finally stop?
If I clasp my knees and try to make my heart rate drop
Will the stairs become just stairs again and not a place to wait
For the anger to subside and the shouting to abate?
Will you promise not to fight again so I can finally sleep,
Can I once more go to my bed, from which I had to creep?
I hear your shouts, they pain me more than you could ever know,
I hold my head upon my knees and pray the noise will go.
Do you not know that when you fight, it's my heart that you shred?
Please stop the fight, just for tonight, so I can go to bed.

Annie Morrice

A New Kitchen

A new kitchen t' pit in, nae buther at a',
but I first ha t'remove the aul units.
So, wi' hammer in hand it's a'going grand,
there a'cumin' oot braw and easy.
But the air's foo o'stoor it's getting worse by the oor
and as it keeps up I'm fair chokin'.
It's lath that I see, o' dearie me,
this is na fit's supposed to happen,
and there's holes in the fleer, that looks gie queer,
nae winder it used to be freezing.
So there's holes in the fleer and the plaster's fa'in' aff,
and the radiator's just sprung a leek,
there's nae cooker, nae gas and nae water iv noo 'cause
there's een or twa things t' be deen.
I'm foonert, I'm hungert, I'm mucket in a',
I really could dee wi a bath.
But at least I've started on i'kitchen
And there's certainly nae turning back.

Rosalind M Walker

SUBURBIA

The London postcode, TW2
Signals they have arrived,
Into the world which they always knew,
Was the only world in which they could survive

Porsche in the driveway, Range Rover too,
Strategically positioned for all to see,
Lunch booked at Harrod's, table for two,
'Someone important wants to meet me.'

Evening at home and champagne on the lawn
With good natured rich folk for company,
Caviar, venison, halibut, prawn,
Maintaining the expected standard is key

And, in the garden to the rear,
Lonely, dishevelled, barely sane,
Distant eyes reflecting fear,
An undernourished dog on a chain.

William McLellan

THE TURBINES

The day is bright and breezy,
We'll go out in the car,
Take a picnic with us,
The beach is not that far.
It's such a lovely afternoon,
We've found a pretty spot,
We spread our goodies on the ground,
Gosh, we've brought a lot.
Sitting down we look around
At the lovely view,
But what I see just spoils my day,
I'm sure it would for you.
Standing there like soldiers,
Arms outstretched to catch the wind,
All the turbine windmills,
These planners they have sinned.
You used to see the mountains
Far as the eye could see,
Now all we see are turbines,
From one to twenty-three.

Trish Elliott

THE ABSENCE OF LOVE

When the pale streaks that are our tears
Plough furrows on the face of the world,
When the entrails boil and seethe
Within this hot ballon in which we whirl,
Languishing wounded, we try to stop our ears
Against the rattling of cruel jewellery
And the roaring waterfall of our fears.

When the sun lifts above the mist on the polder
And dawn stretches and yawns once more,
Cows' heads float on the ether
And another day opens the door,
I can feel myself grow a few hours older
As they grey of age leaks from the black.
Dying a little, gate hinges screech
And bodies lose heat, grow slack.

L Finlayson

ADVICE TO A NEW RECRUIT

If ever you hunt with the Cheshire set
You're in for quite a treat
They're not the best in the land just yet
But don't miss the Boxing Day meet

Half the field will end up tiddled
On the opening glasses of punch
Pray the jumps won't need to be fiddled
And stay away from the bunch

Who's that chap on the ugly black nag?
You don't need to place a wager
If he's rattling money in a bag
It's bound to be the Major

The Pony Club will close the gates
Just wear your very best habit
You surely won't have long to wait
Before they catch a rabbit

Don't let your horse ever kick a hound
And never go any faster
Cos if you do, you're homeward bound
Should you overtake the Master

When day is done you know of course
You'll be heading for your box
With muddy clothes, a sweaty horse
Without catching a single fox.

Christine Skeer

THE LITTLE CHURCH

You little church with walls so strong.
You have stood there many years defying right from wrong.
With steeple oh so grand,
A wonderful structure that will always stand.

Your bells toll for all to hear,
Calling people from far and near.
Sending messages of comfort and calm,
Asking all to attend the service and psalm.

Within your aisles and pews so neat
With altars, candles and flowers a treat,
People and priest with heads bowed in prayer,
Hoping the presence of God is in there.

Deep in their hearts with longing and love
They feel the peace from God up above,
Guiding their lives with a light oh so bright,
Leading their souls from dark into light.

Little church, the comfort you have given,
May all your parishioners be forgiven,
Of all they may unknowingly have done wrong,
With the angels carrying their prayers into song.

As all their hopes rise up above,
May you all be filled with heavenly love.
Let the spirit of all that is peace and content
Make your heart and soul reflect on a life well spent.

Pauline Caton

PUPPY'S THOUGHTS

Please give a thought
before I am bought,
for I'm only a puppy
and I'll have to be taught.

I'm vulnerable you see,
so responsible you'll have to be.
For instance, I'll need a nice clean bed
to rest my tiny head.
Oh! And not forgetting I'll have to be fed.

A walk would be nice,
preferably once, or twice.
When you're away, at home I'll stay,
which is no fun when all you want to do is play.

I wish I could talk,
But I can only walk.
So remember my plea, for you have to see that I have feelings too,
and if you have not, then please don't buy me.

I am for life, so please bear this in mind,
or you'll cause nothing but strife,
as I am for life.

Rita Rogers

SOMBRE THOUGHTS

As I meditate alone at night
How can I presume, to have the right
To hope that life won't pass me by
Without giving me a chance to try.
To find someone just like me
Looking for some company
To share their thoughts, to share their mind
To delve and seek and maybe find
Some simple fact, something to share
A similar feeling that we both could care
About such things, that brings to life
The insanity of war and strife
Why kill and maim for the sake of greed
Making suffering for those in need
It's kindness and love that should abound
Where poverty and filth are all around
Some nations try to help with aid
But all too soon good intentions fade
And what could have been a solid base
Fades away to be another case,
Of a failing, ailing, human race.

D T Pendit

Missing Mistress

There's no one in the bed to greet,
When I come in with muddy feet,
No nice clean clothes for me to smear,
Because the postman's nearly here.
No one to love when she comes in,
With stupid, goofy, toothy grin.
No one to hug, jump at or fuss,
So no use going to meet the bus.
No one to frown, no one to scold,
When I don't do as I am told.
You see, I've got no guarantee,
That you'll be coming back to me
And tho' Dad says I mustn't fret
It seems so long since last we met.
I wait each morning and I wish
There'd be some muesli in my dish.
No one to tell me to be good
When I wake up the neighbourhood
I just don't get it. Where are you?
Where've you gone? I wish I knew!

Paul Bracken

THE BULLY POEM

My mummy takes me into school
Where the biggest, fiercest bullies rule.
After a kick and a mighty punch
I'm counting the seconds until it's lunch
Feeling like a volcano when it erupts its fire
Then a scratch scars my arm as if they'd used a wire
Then playtime comes near
My thoughts fill with fear
Of all the things they do to me
I wish so hard that they would leave me be
Finally the bell goes off
Crying and weary and a non-stop cough.
Another name call from one of the bullies
Now they're trying to push me into the gullies
They never get told off, ooh it's not fair
None of them like me and they certainly don't care
Nobody's perfect especially them
So why do they get the kindness award grade ten!
I'll have to go now I have done enough
They're a bunch of street gangsters and they are all of a scruff!
They will probably cast a spell on me and turn me into a toad.

Elizabeth Marsay (8)

ROMAN FORT

Gleaming eagle glowing,
No fear the Romans are showing.
As they march into battle
With a Celt who's left his cattle
To invade the Roman fort.
Fiercely he flings stones at the army,
But soon he realises it is barmy,
So he runs away,
And he will never come another day.
The barracks are where the soldiers sleep,
And also where they keep
Their glimmering helmets on their beds,
Where they rest their tired heads.
After a day of throwing spears at sacks,
Which they are pretending are the Celts' backs,
They make oil lamps,
So they can see in their camps.

Laura Thompson (10)

THE WIND OF CHANGE

The wind blew wild in the woods today
Reminded me of someone not far away
It enveloped me, excited me, made my heart race
Brought out a picture in my mind, I saw your face
It caressed my body, and ruffled my hair
I thought I were dreaming, I thought you were there
There was a rushing sound, then gentle and calm
I felt the hands of love, wrap around my arm
Do you want one more embrace, was this wind you?
Don't hold back, I need comfort too
The leaves are our children, one, two, three, four.
There's a leaf missing, there should have been one more
I thought of the words that woman at the fair, said to you
At your side there's a little girl, smiling, eyes so blue
Her soul in your keeping, carried gently and with care
I've lost you both, but I feel love in the air
The wind is going away now, it's destiny no one knows
But I'm glad I was there, when the wind blows.

John Hoyland

BUTTERFLIES AND DRAGONFLIES

On a lovely summer's day
When an August sun shines,
Butterflies and dragonflies play,
All dressed up to the nines.

Pretty, dainty butterflies,
Light as a whisper, too:
They gently fall, then they rise,
Silky rainbow coat new.

Bobbing up and down on air,
Dragonflies shimmer like dew.
Their wings are a fairytale pair,
Bodies of every hue.

Belonging to nature and us,
They're pleasure on wings.
Just being, without a fuss,
As each to its life clings.

J Millington

BEATEN BY THE BULLY

Strange faces, strange voices
People who I do not know
Why do they bully me, making me feel so hurt and low
As if it is their pleasure
Making me cry and look so sad
But showing not a care in the world
And bragging that they're glad
I try to hide away, pretending I don't care
To me all this nastiness is just so hard to bare
I'm trying to please and do my best
Wanting to prove myself in life's ongoing test
I want to stay strong and not be afraid
Holding onto hope that this sadness will fade
Awakening in the morning, regretting another day
Discomfort in my memory, as I remember what they say
When the months pass by
I hope for better times
Because I'm the innocent victim
Of their horrible, wicked crimes.

Amanda Louise Marie Clarke

THE D-DAY SOUVENIR SUPPLEMENT

A group of young 'Tommies' clowning for the record.
Way too young, and skinny in their stiff new kit
Laughing and waving with gap-toothed grin,
But a boy at the front isn't really joining in.

'Come on lads you'll be front page news tomorrow'
And his smile for the camera just a rictus on his face.
You sense something in his eyes - not quite fear, not quite sorrow,
That all the boyish larking cannot quite erase.

They should have been back home instead,
In one of many villages or towns,
Where mums and dads and sweethearts would lie worrying a'bed
And wonder what the day would bring for Charlie, Edward, Ted.

Perhaps that's just what he was thinking,
As he knelt down at the front.
He couldn't quite join in with all that banter and bravado,
Because he sensed that come tomorrow,
His first visit to that land
Would have him playing hide and seek with 'Fritz'
                            before dying in the sand.

I leave the photo in the paper on my seat inside the train.
There's been some trouble with the points and I'm late for work again
There's no signal on my mobile so I cannot phone ahead.
The things that 'come to try' us sound so petty when they're said.
When the things that came to try them,
Sixty years since meant - 'You're dead!'

Jane Hinchcliff

TIMOR DESCENDI

Fear of falling keeps her trapped,
nowadays she rarely ventures out after six o'clock.

For with a broken rib or hip,
survival chances slip.
Add broken confidence to the pot
and this vicious circle gathers moss.
As her mobility decreases,
farewell's bid to surefootedness,
then falling risk increases.

It seems fear of the danger is as great,
fear of the danger is as real, as the danger itself,

> *timor descendi -*
>   decline
>   from
>   which
>   there is
>   no return.

Sheila Anderson

BACK HOME UP NORTH

We came back up north, we thought, as a test
To see if the change would be for the best.
Would it bring back the sanity that London sent west
Of the family that went to live down south.

If we seem strange, if our actions seem queer,
If we look like wandering fools, never fear.
We're perfectly harmless, that's why we came here.
On release from our time down south!

If we do things which seem senseless to you
You'll find there's method in all that we do
We're marvels at catching trains, and standing in queues
They teach you all that down south!

And if we look lost in some field or a street
With cap in hand, and a bag at our feet
Pity us kindly, and say, 'It's not reet!'
They've spent too long down south.

Watch us tenderly, treat us with care
We're part of a crowd sent to work down there
To live with the millions, but who wait to cheer
As we leave the masses down south.

And if, when we die, we're sent for a spell,
To some place where souls are made clean and well
We'll pray to Peter to send us to Hell,
And not send us back down south!

Brian Williams

HOMELESS - NOT USELESS

I wander round town all day
Got no money, no place to stay
Trouble at home with my step-dad
His ranting and raving just drove me mad
Can't get a job, can't get a house
I feel dirty, feel like a louse
I don't do drugs, I'm not that kind
I don't want to blow my mind
I have to steal, I need some food
Please Lord forgive me for not being good
If someone could see the good in my heart
Give me a chance, just get a start
I'd do well, was clever at school
I admit I was hasty, young and a fool
Teenagers think they are smart and know all
I know I did then, I had to fall
I'm twenty-two now, I want in from the cold
I'd rather die now than have this when I'm old
So I'm begging you - someone I'm down on my knees
Help me, trust in me please, please, please.

A Sorley

LITTLE BIT OF HEAVEN

We have a little caravan
It's by the River Usk,
In it we feel happy
And smile from dawn to dusk.

It cost a lot of money,
Most of what we had,
But when we're going to it
It makes us all feel glad.

There we do the sort of things
We do not do at home,
Like holding hands and talking
Not sitting on your own.

Sometimes we have a picnic,
Where the ground is flat,
And wonder at the hills
Surrounding where we're sat.

And should the river flood,
As it is prone to do,
We'll call up our insurance
And ask them to renew.

Nigel W Davies

EXTENDED SUMMERTIME IN ORTON

Between the bridges little boats sailed down all day -
No jobs to do and Jean had come to play.
On the breeze the heady lupin scent,
How carelessly those hours were spent.
When the beck ran slow in the heat of the day,
By a shady ledge the minnows lay.

The three small children were playing still,
When the sun sank early behind the hill.
Then, just before the hour was struck,
Came Gladys calling, 'Duck! Duck! Duck!'
With raucous cries the ducks came hurrying,
Under the bridges scurrying, scurrying
In answer to their evening call
And squabbled through the backyard wall
Then, when on mash they'd duly fed,
Went off to grumble in their shed.

In the twilight hardly a sound at all.
Murmurs from the den behind the wall.
Perhaps Mam might just forget to call.

I wonder are children still playing now?
Do ducks swim where the monkey musks grow?
In the heat of the day, when the beck runs slow,
By Town End Bridge do minnows go?
As shadows lengthen and the damp dusk looms low
Up the garth by the house do glow-worms still glow?

Eileen Todd

TRAVELLERS' JOY

When you travel in this county
In the early days of June,
Should you chance on an encampment
On the banks say, by the Lune.

Here are not those New Age Travellers
You can bet your very boots.
These be on an annual journey
And they stem from earlier roots.

Soon the horses and the wagons
Will be back upon their way,
On Appleby their sights are fixed
To reach perhaps this day.

In a massive camp upon 'The Hill',
Old friends will make a deal,
Showing off their horse's paces.
Shaking hands a bond to seal.

Artistic wagons on display
Are not all daily homes.
Now living vans all spick and span
Have ornate glass and chromes.

Brisk trade there'll be in horses,
And in the harness tack.
All nomads' needs are catered for
Before they travel back.

Their week will soon have come and gone,
A good time had by all.
Then farewell for another year,
The highway keeps its call.

R G Males

THE MASK

A mask is a wonderful thing to wear,
To hide from the world all your fears and care,
Sometimes so big you can see no end,
Others so small they easily mend.

A child at school has many fears
But must not admit to shedding tears
So she puts on her mask to make her bold
And appears to her friends extremely cold.

An actress, a dancer, a singer, a player,
For that first performance, a mask she must wear,
To hide her knees that tremble when standing
In front of an audience, pleasure demanding.

A mourner, showing her great devotion,
Feels she must speak without emotion,
Puts on a mask to hide her feeling
When with the rest of the world she's dealing.

At last, when all her friends depart,
She takes off the mask and breaks her heart,
She goes to her room, in deep despair
And cries to God to hear her prayer.

Our army, our navy, our airmen, so brave,
All wear their masks to help them behave,
In this terrible war to fight as they must
Amongst bombs and guns and sand and dust.

Under their masks they are young and kind,
Wanting to put all this cruelty behind,
And return to their loved ones, waiting at home,
Where they can take off their masks and in freedom roam.

Nicola Preston (15)

THE HEEBIE JEEBIES

Treating every sound with suspicion,
With fears that won't go away.
Invisible ghosts on the periphery of vision
As senses do their best to betray.

With fears that won't go away,
Heightened by the state I'm in.
As senses do their best to betray,
They have me jumping out of my skin.

Heightened by the state I'm in,
Invisible ghosts on the periphery of vision.
They have me jumping out of my skin
Treating every sound with suspicion.

Keith Tissington

SOLAR DESIRE

Daytime is over, I dream at the window
Oh me! Oh my! What is that I spy?
The brazen eve sun stoops low,
And kisses the old fir tree!
The fir, once commonplace evergreen,
Now flushes bronze and rust,
To the tips of its needles is burnished all over
Surprised by the setting sun's lust,
A momentary flare of solar desire
Bursts through the copse like wildfire.

Elizabeth M Rait

TAKE A LOOK AROUND

Take a look around
What do you see?
Pain and suffering is what's clear to me
Kids unaware of the dangers
Of familiar faces not just complete strangers
While the simple folks only think about fictional babies in mangers

The only news is bad news
From distant tragedies to the persecution of Jews
All they do is moan about violence being glorified
While we celebrate those who fight and mourn those who died
Immortalising people for doing what's wrong
Remembering their 'triumphs' long after they've gone

How can we raise our children in a life like this?
When all we have is chaos and without a pot to piss
Children brought up in broken homes
While we spend billions on war and millennium domes
Mothers too busy chasing dragons
While fathers are carted off in meat wagons

So take a look around
All I see is people dying
People crying
While the rest of us remain oblivious
To the blatantly obvious
Life ain't perfect, it's far from it
So take my life, cos I don't want it.

Craig Stewart

PURPLE SKIRT

You said I was lovely in my purple skirt
And you promised not to preen and flirt
I left the party for a little while
But when I returned, a girl in a different style
Black trousers, tight top, behind my back
Was hanging sexily around your neck.
Is it as I suspect
Is there something you lack?
Are your love words fancy?
Are you just cheap and chancy?

Margaret McKelvey

You Can't Win 'Em All

The boys were wild; none wore a shirt,
raggedy shorts, bulletproof feet,
the ball was a bundle of tatty rags,
Saturday mornings, they all would meet.
That dusty square on which they played,
flattened for years, by a million souls
corner posts were a couple of sticks,
two piles of stone; marked the goals.
The lads played hard, but always fair,
twenty-a-side and sometimes more,
which side won, it was not known,
nobody bothered about keeping score.

As they played one Saturday morning,
came the sound of marching boots,
freedom fighters lined their pitch,
hoping to abduct, some raw recruits.
They cheered the boys, each time they scored,
roaring encouragement, being kind,
putting the players at their ease,
not letting on, what they had in mind.
After the match, those freedom fighters,
told stories of adventure, glory and fame,
how those lads, could all be heroes, playing the freedom game.

Many of the boys went off freely;
to an away match, they must not fail
mothers were sobbing for their children,
as they left, on that unknown trail
many years passed, they were champions,
and jungle drums beat out the news,
those boys were coming home at last,
it seemed they could never lose.
They fought their final conflict, battling a better team,
government troops slaughtered them,
coming home, was a shattered dream.

The boys were wild no longer;
lying naked, silent and dead.
They might have had, bulletproof feet,
none had a bulletproof head.

Roy Hare

CHASING THE DRAGONS

My torment is that he should be
So distant and apart from me
My son - who brought such joy and tears
Through innocent adolescent years
With aching heart it grieves me so
To see a stranger come and go
Now I look into his soulful eyes
And see the fear he can't disguise
What took him on that journey where
There is no hope - but dark despair?
His own cocoon - a living hell
A place where he seems doomed to dwell
When he comes down from being high
And I listen to his plaintive cry
For all the years that he has lost
In sad withdrawal he counts the cost
The 'Dragon' that he tries to slay
Returns to haunt him every day
So then I pray that he may find
Contentment that brings piece of mind
Released from torment - unchained and free
Back to the world of reality

Carol Kaye

A World For Us All

We're ugly, we're lonely
We're happy, we're sad

We're one of so many
We're good, and we're bad

We all have emotions
Which don't always show

Because of conditions
In which we all grow

Pain is a part of the way which we live
Pleasure is all in the mind

People can often have so much to give
Peace can be so hard to find

No one is equal but now that we're here
The choice is we live or we die

If we just quarrel because we're not clear
We'll find it so hard to get by

We push and we shove and we climb and we fall
In the process of staying alive

Below or above there's a world for us all
If we help one another survive

Nothing is certain but changes that come
And no one is totally free

Life is in motion and we are just some
Of the forms that you're likely to see.

Peter Owen

CIRCUMSTANCES

A girl I left school light-hearted,
And bid my chums a bright adieu,
I wasn't sorry we had parted,
I'd fixed ideas and plans in view,
Alas I found like others many,
You couldn't pick and choose between,
And simply grasped the chance if any,
Way of earning money clean,
Now years have passed, I shouldn't grumble,
Yet I kick the traces still,
That forced me to adoft this humble,
Mode of living, against my will,
Of youthful ambition proudly built,
And castles gilded bright tho' hazy,
For their downfall I can't take guilt,
Blame misdemeanour or being lazy.

If circumstances had decreed,
That this must be my true vocation
That all I ask that I be freed,
From life, perhaps in death salvation.

I Morgan

A House by the Sea
(Man to the hill, woman to the shore. Old Gaelic proverb)

I will build myself a house by the sea
Where the salt-water wind will invigorate me
And the sweep of the bay and the sand and the sky
Will awaken my soul to take wings and fly.

I will build myself a house by the sea
Where the smell of the swell will resuscitate me.
And the young girl inside so long shackled with fears
Will run with the roar of the waves in her ears.

I will build myself a house by the sea
Where bare feet on wet sand will rejuvenate me
And I'll swim by the shore till the sun in the west
Shines her sweet comfort upon my warm breast.

I will build myself a house by the sea
Where the tang of seaweed will animate me
And I'll watch the wild gulls soar high without care
As they ride the fresh breeze in the bright morning air.

I will build myself a house by the sea
Where the tide at full moon will exhilarate me.
And I'll hear the wild geese awaken the dawn
And I'll turn in my sleep and dream on and on.

Brendan McCauley

FAVOURITE THINGS

Smooth stone, soft feather
Days out, holiday weather;
Autumn days and country ways;
Awesome mountains
Glistening fountains;
A babbling brook
A favourite book;
Woolly blankets, nice warm bed
Rainbow colours, especially red!
Clear cool streams
And long sweet dreams;
Rocking chairs and teddy bears;
Warm animal fur
A cat's deep purr;
Home-made pies
And rainwashed skies;
The ocean surf and planet Earth;
A cherub's wings
My favourite things.

Cate Ryan

GOLDEN WONDERS OF GOLD DUST

Tortured heart; tortured mind
So disturbing, so unkind
How to flee from deep distress!
- Feeling one is lacking; less

In *status, gifts* and worthy praise
Despite them toiling; *dismal* days
One was so *worthy* to; had claimed -
That opportunist hope this aimed!

Regrets *galore*, the cause of such
Heart-wrenching ache, of which there's much.
An empty struggle, *made in vain*
To flee the *plight* of mindful pain.

The hope is to one day *forget*
That dark black hole of deep regret,
- The bitter pill of shattered dreams
Is hard to swallow and it seems

One's life will never now hold true
To what it felt was in its due
- The *many* years of hard endeavour
Hard work, hard toil and *being clever*

Gave rise to one a chance to be
A big success of high decree

Alas, it was *not* meant to be
And this one cannot fail to see
'Twas just a milestone, born to fate
Success will just come *sometimes* late!

Kiran Kaur Rana

Two Decades Of Love

Two decades ago,
I let it all go.
The beginning, the start,
Of giving you my heart.

The letters I wrote,
Not just any notes.
The radio messages I left,
All genuine and heartfelt.

Some strange force made us click,
Chemical reaction began to tick.
Destiny set the date,
It had to be fate.

I was innocent, young and pure,
I wanted you, that's for sure.
You are a genuine piece of art,
My childhood sweetheart.

Two decades have passed,
It's gone so fast.
Stomach butterflies from the start,
You still tickle my heart.

The letters I write,
Are meaningful and right.
You make my heart melt,
Still genuine and heartfelt.

The same force we still click,
Chemical reaction still ticks.
Nothing changes you see,
You're still the guy for me.

I'm now divine, wise and mature,
I still want you, that's for sure.
You're my priceless piece of art,
Forever, hold my heart.

Melanie McMahon

BUBBLES

Floating gently through the air
I'm a little bubble without a care,
Softly bouncing up and down,
To the laughter of children all around.

Little faces full of delight
Trying to catch me, without their sight,
Chirps of laughter all around
At my bobbing up and down.

How light am I, and very fragile
One little touch, and I'd be gone
Just a memory, to those around
Of a little bubble, who made no sound.

M Crowder

VELVET MOON

The dark sky, wrapped in her midnight blue coat
Shows off a sprinkling of many a star
They glisten like studded crystals
Precious gems admired from afar

Out in the distance his creamy white face
Smiles as he hugs the lady in blue
The man in the moon has fallen victim
To his diamond clad Beauty; he'll always be true

She adores the softly glowing light
He shines throughout in his pursuit of her
Shamelessly flirting on this night
His sensuality makes her stir

The velvet moon leaves her breathless
His milk and honey sweetness fair
She'll lose her heart to his alluring charm
But they're both aware that they must share

With couples everywhere who kiss
Under her stars and his golden romance
The velvet moon, the lady in blue
Invite all lovers to join their dance.

Marie A Golan

LIFE'S MEMORIES

Within these walls I've known so well
Where joy and laughter used to dwell

Such childly voices rang out with pride
No nook or cranny could sorrow hide

Such flower of youth lived within
Dream and whims of childhood had their fling

Salty tears, and broken wings
Words spoke in haste but never meant

Such other things done to make one's heart content
The love that dwelt within these walls
So many sweet memories to recall

While winter wiles through darkness flow
The warmth of those you've loved still burns

By firelight glow to warmth the heart of those left alone
Who played their part in time now flown

Mary Veronica Ciarella Murray

A Dream

The picture is very scary
And I'm not sure what I see
It's like a scene from Macbeth
But that just cannot be

Three witches sit around the cauldron
Their faces haggard and pale
They cast their spells throughout the night
Despite the wind and hail

The long black cloaks touch the floor
As they huddle and stir
The cauldron bubbles, the mixture spills
And blue smoke fills the air

When I look again the smoke has gone
The witches have vanished too
I realise it was all a dream
None of it was true.

M Lyon

THE DAWNING LIGHT OF LIFE

I watch the dawn come up
Shadows of the night are fading away
Colours of purple, smudged with grey
The beginning of another day
Shadows from the trees, stretch out their branches
Like giant fingers across the sky
Silhouettes in black so stark to my eyes
And here am I looking through my windows, in my room
Wrapped in my solitude
While the world sleeps
My heart aches, my eyes they weep
Loneliness like a silent invader
Seeps into my being
Suddenly the world has changed
Daylight steals its way in
For another day to begin
The first blackbird arrives, searching for food
Just as I search for life's answers
I am confused
By life, with all its tricks, and treachery
A jester's game in all its mockery.

Patricia Johnson

BURNING BARD

Listen to me singing
Listen to me cry
See my body bleeding
See my body die.

I sing of captive existence and drown
In dark wept pools of loneliness
I bleed through veins that tie me down
And dehumanise in my universal emptiness.

Trapped by walls of a clouded past
The music turns to screams
My history comes upon me fast
The nightmare of this life lies dormant in my dreams.

I see my body fade
Beyond the help of good
My journey is delayed
With the face behind the hood.

Scars that tear through my heart
Like a cracked crystal shard
Tyrannic insanity that comes apart
And immortal flames I cannot discard.

Distorted visions flicker in my mind
Those of tortured angels raped by demonic whores
Self-generated futures all leaving me behind
Mortality the sentence given by the unknown laws.

Black angels and white demons blur inside my head
Keeping me off the scales of self-knowledge's pursuit
My eyes becoming liars and all I see is red
As I bathe in Earth's excretions and the stench of rotten fruit.

Lee Tellis Adams

NOSTALGIA

And did our feet (in ancient times)
walk through the hills and fields so green -
and did we play our childish games
without a 'mugger' to be seen -
and did the aeroplanes on high
advertise 'Persil' in the sky -
well, we're still here to prove just why -
it must have been.

B Haworth

AN EMPTY SPACE

Life has nothing whatsoever to contribute to absolution,
I have lied severely each year to create a brand new resolution,
My life form has no qualifications to offer any space or time,
Any angelic qualities ever possessed now bear filth and guilt fed grime,
What sort of place will this be without another life?
Just another place to fill with frustration, guilt and strife,
I have no need to justify my actions,
I covet for some strength,
This noose is all I need and the variation of its length,
Trust no one who will forge a smile for reasons that are unknown,
Stay beautiful in physical form and my legend will have grown,
Never become friends with a soul that will endeavour to lie,
I bid farewell with a heartfelt kiss and the words, 'Goodbye'
When you'll sleep and see my face,
I'm just another 'empty space'

Morgan Galsworthy

THE DAY

The sky above,
The Earth below,
The sunset sets,
The Earth aglow,
The hooting owl,
The twinkling star,
The lowing of
The herd afar.

The lonely lover,
The pining maid,
The words of love,
The vows once made,
The thunder storm,
The scurrying mouse,
The cliff-top hill,
The lovely house.

The crack of dawn,
The graceful fawn,
The rustle of leaves,
On windswept lawn,
The golden sunrise,
The cockerel's crow,
The blazing fire,
The hearth aglow.

T B O'Brien-Barden

WHEN ALL SEEMS LOST

When all seems lost, and you have no place to go
When your burden seems heavy and your head hangs low
Just look around and you will find
Your greatest treasures are in your mind
Remember though, before you start
You may just find, a broken heart
There is always someone, perhaps out there
Who may love you, they may really care
You may find all may not be lost at all
Stand up straight, stand proud and tall
The world out there is no large wall
It may look a mountain that you must climb
You do not reach the top, it is no shame
If the fault is yours, then take the blame
If it is your life you wish to measure
Give your very best, that will be your treasure
Don't worry about what you have not
Just think of the things that you have got
Take this opportunity while you are still here
Reach for the moon, you have nothing to fear
When all seems lost look at the stars above
Then who knows, you may find true love

Francis McGarry

ANNIHILATION

A tortoise without a shell
A skunk with no smell
A rabbit scurrying,
              Not staying perfectly still
A stag of bright colours,
              Illuminated,
                          Out on the hill
And out in the road,
              A wee flattened form
The hedgehog;
      His prickles;
             His tight ball;
                    Gone.
            His body;
                    Savagely torn.
And what of ourselves?
Where are our shells?
Where is *my* shell?
Will I spill out;
              Become too much?
Do perfumes sweet
          Invite bees to sting?
Does standing still
          Invite the kill?
Held by the throat
          Shaken in hate
A heart no longer beating
            A flame extinguished
                        A spirit suspended.
            Annihilation!

Nancy Black

Jake

With you unseen friends you happily play,
fantasising little child,
your imagination so wild,
for you yet another perfect day,
they hide, you seek, you find.

The purity of your immature mind,
innocent little boy,
with a manner so coy,
for you I pray life will be kind,
and your laughter not destroy.

D Brown

WELCOME HOME

I look at the picture
And what do I see
A welcome home banner
From your family

A son has returned
From a place far away (Pennsylvania),
Where teaching young children
Was part of his day

The banner says, 'Welcome home Steve'
In my heart I say don't leave
But very soon you were on your way
To teach older children not so far away

We kept the banner
For old times sake
In an old shoe box
For a treasured keepsake

Dilys Hallam

BOAT PEOPLE

Pamper then share a hamper
Put on a jumper
Do another romp
Finale, sing a song of peace

Provide correct answers
On square paper
Make ends meet
Cover job teach the Boat People please

Search for a clue
Sink into the morning dew
Fold away old newspapers
Altogether a good innings - sport!

S M Thompson

As I Grow Older

As I grow older, years rushing past,
My memory harkens back,
To innocent days, gentler ways, when I was but a lass.

Did the summers really last that long?
Did the sun's glow shine brighter then?
Did the snow in winter drift so high?
Or does my mind play tricks again?

Village life was all I knew,
Home from school, run fast,
To farmer's field where Dad was working,
Harvest hay, stacked at last.

Milk was delivered by horse and cart,
By Farmer Rufus and his old mare Phil,
Ladled from churn, to Mum's old jug,
He charged but 1/2d a gill.

Hand me down clothes, make-do, and mend,
Didn't expect anymore,
Ration book living, was all we knew,
Co-op divi, Lord's day for the poor.

No telly, computer or CDs for us,
All todays must have inventions,
We hadn't been programmed; to buy, buy, buy,
As the young of today are, no question.

Dorothy M Mitchell

THANK YOU FOR CARING FOR US

We tell all our family and friends
It's worth always keeping in touch.
We miss you by living in Jersey but
Look forward to seeing you so much

Thank you for praying and writing;
We do love to read all your news.
Most of all, thank you for photos
To remind us you're caring for us.

Francesca Winson

Goodnight My Love

With tired eyes, and a body which aches
A mind full of problems, with no exit or place,
She pulls back the cover, sweet thoughts fill her mind,
The comfort of her bed, and eyes so fine.

The welcome of dark, embrace the warmth of her heart,
Crisp cotton sheets, with subconscious apart.
Her mind letting go, the muscles slowly relax,
The visions so crystal, rapid eye movement, happiness . . . 'attacks'

A figurine outline, the crease shapes her lay
The rise of the cover, dreaming an array
While you sleep tonight, a simple prayer to you,
May your dreams be blissful, not making you blue.

Mark Spiller

BEING IN HOSPITAL FOR THE MENTALLY ILL

Life is good, life is fast,
You must forget about your past,
If you don't it'll make you ill,
They'll put you in hospital,
They'll give you pills,
You cry and cry but they don't care,
You're so depressed
Won't even let you out for air.
They come to your bed
They look at you,
You feel like an animal in the zoo,
They know you're ill but they don't care,
They drug you up no time to spare,
Making their job easy that's all they care,
They drugged me up so much, so much,
I could not walk, talk or touch,
They talk to you like you are s**t,
Because we are ill they get away with it,
If we were to answer back they'd give you
                            a needle up the jack,
They never make no time to talk,
Won't even let you out for walks,
Now I've been there, now I know,
I feel so sorry for other people that have to go.
They should get new staff that treat you well,
Not just like a little girl.
They should get new staff who have a laugh
With you instead of treating you like
                caged animals in the zoo.

Joanne Owen

SHATTERED IMAGE

Look at me
What do you see?
Not me I guess
Look deep and there I am
Buried beneath the mockery called Man
Kind and gentle that's me
Not macho and ego driven see
Sorry if this is not what you want
But no one ever thought to ask me
Is this my life I see laid before me,
Or is it the life from which the world
Would have me live?
Forced I am to live a lie
Trapped deep within
That is where I lie
Not on the outside
This is why I am forced to keep up
This shattered illusion of Man.

Tosky

Poorly Enriching Sweetener

Stop! I ain't no paramedic or professional ballerina
just a ditched anaemic trucker suffering from emphysema

Stop! I ain't no tick-taper or demonic hit parader
I'm a feverish mosaic wailing like a dumb narrator

Stop! I ain't no psychedelic or this valiant canary
my geography is lost in the throes of Londonderry

Stop! I ain't no Charlie Chaplin or a Goddess of wild beatniks
wondering whatever happened to the poorly enriching sweetener

This is really what creates the taste of momentary pleasure
dimming all of future brightness by rubbing shoulders with
Queen Leisure - shadowy in every way as if to paraphrase
the operatics dedicated to the days when I was central to affray

Stop! I ain't no paramedic or besotted ballerina
nor that glorious romantic in profoundly sexy gear!

Steven Ilchev

LIGHT TRANSCENDING

I follow you through paths forged of the stars.
I labour ever on even though I am weary
And the wings I found to fly have faltered so many times
And the tiredness has nearly overcome me
And the desire to lie down beckons at the door.
I follow you because my heart is not big enough to forgive if I lie down
Because the tiredness reminds me that I am awake
Because these wings of mine are too beautiful to surrender,
I follow because in the choices that I have
I have no choice.

They follow me in their droves and their clusters
Radiating out their love, their fear,
Their whispers carry me forth on their greatness
A greatness I have not the strength to withhold
And they come now in utter ignorance, in bliss, in perfection,
For the brightness they see they cannot ignore
This is their beacon, this is my starburst,
They follow me, they have no choice at all.

Samantha Cumes

TINY ALIEN

Sailing on a flake of snow
Drifting silently to Earth I go;
Earthlings can't see me, I'm so small
They don't even know I've arrived at all.
It's fun making house calls,
I've no need of a key,
Entering through keyholes is easy for me.
Hitching rides I travel everywhere,
I'm a tiny alien without a care.
In a perambulator I went for a ride,
Baby and I cosily slept side by side.
Feeling hungry I ate a crumb of cake,
Alas, it gave me a tummy ache.
A cheeky spider pulled my leg
So I gave him a thump on the head.
I'm going for a long flight tomorrow
On the back of a friendly sparrow.

Audrey Luckhurst

Past, Present, Future

You were the inspiration
Behind the first words written
A tiny spark that ignited
And slowly grew into passion.

You are the inspiration
Cradled in my heart
The flickering flame that warms
Both brain and body.

You will be the inspiration
Encouraging ever onward
The raging fire that will flow
Through pen and paper.

Lynne Gilbert

WORDS

Words that are spoken can say so much
as they send out powerful vibes,
that touch the part of our mind and heart
sometimes brings on sighs.

Words that are spoken in jest,
can often lead to tears,
even though they are not meant seriously
our thoughts can become unclear.

They also bring joy and laughter
and quite suddenly too,
just one words can fetch a smile,
that stem from me and you.

Words can bring us happiness,
and help to quell our fears,
expressions that are so important,
all through our living years.

Rhoda Starkey

INFORMATION

We hope you have enjoyed reading this book - and that you will continue to enjoy it in the coming years.

If you like reading and writing poetry drop us a line, or give us a call, and we'll send you a free information pack.

Alternatively if you would like to order further copies of this book or any of our other titles, then please give us a call or log onto our website at www.forwardpress.co.uk

**Anchor Books Information
Remus House
Coltsfoot Drive
Peterborough
PE2 9JX
(01733) 898102**